ALSO BY LEE SIEGEL

⤙·⤚

Falling Upwards: Essays in Defense of the Imagination

Not Remotely Controlled: Notes on Television

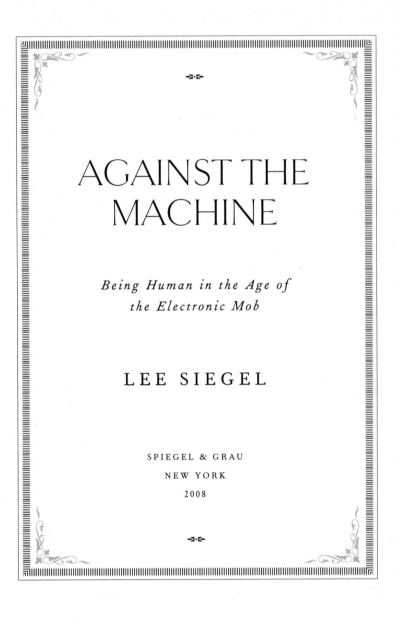

AGAINST THE MACHINE

*Being Human in the Age of
the Electronic Mob*

LEE SIEGEL

SPIEGEL & GRAU

NEW YORK

2008

PUBLISHED BY SPIEGEL & GRAU

Copyright © 2008 by Lee Siegel

Published in the United States by Spiegel & Grau, a division of
Random House, Inc., New York.

www.spiegelandgrau.com

SPIEGEL & GRAU is a trademark of Random House, Inc.

Book design by Ellen Cipriano

Library of Congress Cataloging-in-Publication Data
Siegel, Lee, 1957–
Against the machine : being human in the age of the electronic mob /
Lee Siegel. —1st ed.
p.   cm.
1. Information technology—Social aspects. 2. Cyberspace—Social aspects.
3. Internet—Social aspects. 4. Subculture. 5. Popular culture.
6. Computers and civilization. I. Title.
HM851.S5484 2008
303.48'33—dc22
2007027694

ISBN 978-0-385-52265-6

PRINTED IN THE UNITED STATES OF AMERICA

1   3   5   7   9   10   8   6   4   2

First Edition

For Julian

CONTENTS

❧PART THREE❧

Introduction

THIS BOOK IS ABOUT the way the Internet is reshaping our thoughts about ourselves, other people, and the world around us. It's also about the way the Internet itself has grown out of changes in society and culture. I had been wanting to write it for years, yet the book's origins don't lie in the Internet. They lie in a belief that, for better or worse, has guided my life as a writer, and especially as a cultural critic. Things don't have to be the way they are.

Consider the automobile, like the Internet one of the more marvelous inventions of humankind. By the early 1960s, however, fifty thousand people were dying in car accidents every year. Among other reasons for the high rate of fatalities, transmissions were hard to operate, the use of chrome and other brightly reflective materials inside the cars made it hard for drivers to see, and there were no protective restraints to keep passengers from being hurled through the windshield in a crash. Yet the public didn't complain. The rhetoric surrounding the automobile had made it impervious to skepticism. Cars were not just a marvel of convenience, people were told, they were a miracle of social and personal transformation.

Advertising identified the car's power and mobility with the promise of American life itself. The car's speed made any criticism seem fuddy-duddy and reactionary. So did the fact that changing automobile styles functioned as the visual embodiment of a particular year. The "make" of your car was the very definition of your social relevance as its owner. Cars moved so fast and their styles changed so fast that they acquired the illusion of an eternal condition, like the revolving of the seasons.

Such an illusion gave auto manufacturers a pretext for their neglect. They could hide their cost-conscious refusal to make cars safer behind their claim that nothing could be done—the trade-off in human life was inevitable and inexorable. That was the nature of cars. What's more, cars empowered the individual to an unprecedented degree. The increasingly affordable automobile seemed like the ultimate proof and fulfillment of democracy. If people were dying on the road in greater numbers, it was because greater numbers of people were enjoying the freedom, choice, and access provided by the new machines roaring along the open road. Criticize the car and you were criticizing democracy. Anyway, that's just the way things were.

Until 1965. That was the year Ralph Nader published *Unsafe at Any Speed,* his classic exposé of the automobile industry's criminal neglect. The public was horrified. It seemed that auto industry executives had known all along what the problems were. Engineers had pressed them to make changes that would have saved tens of thousands of lives, but the bosses silenced the criticism for the sake of cutting costs and protecting the shareholders and their own jobs.

Not only was the public horrified; it was shocked. What it had accepted as an inevitable condition turned out to be wholly arbitrary. Things should have been very different from the way they were. And gradually, by means of public pressure, the "permanent" condition of the necessarily dangerous car did yield to the new condition of a safety-conscious auto industry. People stopped dying on the road in staggering numbers. Things changed.

Heaven knows, I'm not comparing the Internet to a hurtling death trap. But the Internet has its destructive side just as the automobile does, and both technologies entered the world behind a curtain of triumphalism hiding their dangers from critical view. Like the car, the Internet has been made out to be a miracle of social and personal transformation when it is really a marvel of convenience—and in the case of the Internet, a marvel of convenience that has caused a social and personal upheaval. As with the car, the highly arbitrary way in which the Internet has evolved has been portrayed as inevitable and inexorable. As with the car, criticism of the Internet's shortcomings, risks, and perils has been silenced, or ignored, or stigmatized as an expression of those two great American taboos, negativity and fear of change. As with the car, a rhetoric of freedom, democracy, choice, and access has covered up the greed and blind self-interest that lie behind what much of the Internet has developed into today.

Now, you would have to be a fool to refuse to acknowledge that the Internet is a marvel of convenience. Google, Amazon, and Nexis saved me months of research and title hunting while writing this book. Recently, the Internet enabled my family and me to find an apartment in perhaps one-fourth the time it would have taken in pre-Internet days. Without some trustworthy medical Web sites, my wife and I would have spent countless more nights worrying over our infant son during the first weeks of his life. Without e-mail, it might even have taken me longer to meet my wife, or to have a career as a writer! I sometimes speak haltingly, and shyly. E-mail made it possible for me to pursue work and love in the medium in which I, as a writer, feel most comfortable.

No one can deny the Internet's capacity to make life easier, smoother, and more pleasant. But let's be honest. I would have installed myself at the library and made the rounds of used-book stores, and eventually written this book without the Internet. My family and I would have found an apartment. A few extra trips to the doctor would have spared us anxiety about our little boy. Work and love would not have eluded me even if I had had to rely on the spoken rather than the written word. Without the Internet, all these things would have been accomplished, or they would have ironed themselves out. The Internet made one big difference. Everything worked itself out more quickly and efficiently. More conveniently.

Convenience is an essential part of what most contemporary commercial propositions promise to bring us. Yet commerce and convenience exist not for their own sake, but to make life more meaningful outside the arena of commerce. No one's epitaph ever read: "Here Lies Mr. Cavanaugh, Who Led a

Convenient Life, and Made Life Convenient for Others." And yet in the name of convenience, the Internet has been declared a revolution on a par with the invention of the printing press.

The Internet, however, is completely unlike the printing press. Spreading knowledge through books has nothing to do with buying books online. Spreading knowledge to people who lack it has nothing to do with the Internet's more rapid dispersal of information that is already available. And giving everyone "a voice," as the Internet boosters boast of having done, is not only very different from enabling the most creative, intelligent, or original voices to be heard. It can also be a way to keep the most creative, intelligent, and original voices from being heard.

The sometimes hysterical claims over the past few years that the Internet is an epoch-making revolution in social and personal relations follow the same arc. They always go on to describe the "revolution" in commercial terms of general consumer empowerment. In terms of convenience. But a revolution in convenience cannot possibly be—as precious a quality as convenience is nowadays—anything that can be called a revolution. And yet the Internet has indeed caused a revolution. It's just that the prophets of the Internet don't ever want to talk about what type of revolution it is.

The Internet as technical innovation is the answer to our contemporary condition of hectic, disconnected, fragmented activity. A century of technological change has filled our busy days with near-simultaneous disparate experiences. Being online now allows us to organize these experiences, almost to unify them. (What is "compartmentalization" but a way to keep several "windows" open at the same time?) Despite our lamentations that e-mail is running and ruining our lives, we can keep up, in some type of manageable fashion, with the accelerated rhythms of clashing life spheres.

In the same way, the Internet's social and psychological nature is the answer to a century of social and psychological change. During that time, the individual was gradually elevated above society. Satisfying our own desires has become more important than balancing our relationships with other people.

The age of Freud, the Existential Self, the Therapeutic Self, the Confessional Self, the Performing Self, the age of the memoir, the Me Generation, the Culture of Narcissism—life has become more mentalized, more inward, more directed toward the gratification of personal desire. The collapse of the family and the preponderance of people living alone are aspects of this trend; tragically, so is the shocking frequency of violence, even of mass murder, in public places. We live more in our own heads than any society has at any time, and for some people now the only reality that exists is the one inside their heads.

This is not a condemnation of how we live. Community in the form of pernicious ideologies and destructive tribalisms has created more misery than radical individualism ever did. There's much to be said for our isolated, separate lives, for the greater "access" they provide to a broader array of pleasures and protections. But however our present condition develops, the Internet offers the first cohesive social and psychological framework for this relatively new condition. The Internet is the first social environment to serve the needs of the isolated, elevated, asocial individual.

In the sense that the Internet responds to a set of conditions that have been many decades in the making, it is an inevitable technological development. But the nature of the Internet, once it had been invented, was not, and is not, inevitable. Technology is neutral, value-free, neither inherently good nor bad. Values are what make technology either an aid or an obstacle to human life.

We shop, play, work, love, search for information, seek to communicate with each other and sometimes with the world online. We spend more time alone than ever before. Yet people are not arguing about the effects of this startling new condition.

Occasionally, alarms are sounded about identity theft, addictive behavior, or the sexual exploitation of children online. These are real dangers, especially the online sexual war against children. But they are only the most extreme, and the most visible, hazards of the world of the Internet. They will eventually be brought under control by legislation, courts, and committees. And anyway, such concerns are usually dismissed as hysteria, in the same way that worrying about the high rate of traffic deaths was once dismissed as hysteria. If people are being preyed upon online in greater numbers, we are told, it's because greater numbers of people are enjoying the freedom, choice, and access provided by the new machines propelling us into open, infinite cyberspace. That is the nature of the Internet.

The Internet magnifies these pathological patterns of behavior, but it didn't create them. What cannot be resolved by legislation, courts, and committees are patterns of behavior created by the Internet itself, problems spawned by the Internet's everyday routines. But fundamental questions about the Internet's new conventions almost never get asked. Instead, the public gets panels of like-minded Internet boosters—and investors—outdoing each other in singing the Internet's praises. Anyone who does challenge Internet shibboleths gets called fuddy-duddy or reactionary. Criticize the Internet and you are accused of criticizing democracy. The triumphal, self-congratulating rhetoric surrounding the Internet has made it impervious to criticism.

Strangest of all, although skepticism is journalism's stock-in-trade, newspaper and magazine editors are more reluctant than anyone else to make substantial criticisms of the Internet. This, despite the fact that mainstream journalism is the Internet boosters' most popular target. The financial pressures on the editors of newspapers and magazines, and their fears of being superseded by the new medium, have crippled their skeptical instincts.

Establishment paralysis certainly contributed to the imbroglio I found myself in a year and a half ago, when as a staff writer at the *New Republic* I encountered anonymous commenters in the Talkback section of the culture blog I had been invited to write for the magazine: "Mr. Siegal [*sic*] came onto many peoples [*sic*] sanctuary, pissed in the urns, farted and then put his dick upon the altar"; "Siegel is a retarded mongoloid"; "Siegel wanted to fuck a child." I couldn't understand how a serious magazine could allow these things to appear, and written by people who were concealing their true identities to boot. Understandably daunted by the "new" media's insistence on "open discussion," the *New Republic* had decided against enforcing its new Talkback section's Rules of Use, which prohibited "posts that are defamatory, libelous, unnecessarily antagonistic . . . posts that are obscene, abusive, harassing, threatening, off-topic, unintelligible, or inappropriate." But these were good, sound rules that in fact encouraged open discussion. And my mother was reading this stuff, for goodness' sake! Worst of all, whatever appears on the Web stays on the Web. Forever.

So after futilely protesting such a ridiculous situation to the editors (and later polemicizing on my blog against what I called "thuggish anonymity" and the practice of deception on the Internet, which was like blowing smoke rings at a firing squad), I decided that since I had fallen through the looking glass into some surreal landscape, I might as well have a little fun, get down in the mud, and give thuggish anonymity a taste of thuggish anonymity. I called myself "sprezzatura" (a term coined during the Italian Renaissance that connotes a deceptive simplicity), celebrated the despicable Mr. Siegel, and attacked his incontinent attackers in their own idiom. That, I naively thought, would show them.

My prank discovered, I was temporarily suspended by a terrified *New Republic*, pilloried by the blogosphere (as a representative example of the Internet's capacity for thuggish anonymity and deceit!), denounced by the mainstream media, and then, in good American fashion, rewarded with an interview in the *New York Times Magazine* and the opportunity to write the book on Web culture that I'd long wanted to write. In the wake of the scandal, articles that worried about malicious anonymity on the Internet began to appear in the *Guardian*, the *Nation, Salon*, the *New York Times*, and the *New Republic* itself. Up to that point, the convention of anonymous attacks in the blogosphere had rarely been challenged. But gradually, the articles for the most part stopped appearing, and the culture of the Internet again went mostly unexamined and unquestioned.

This book is not about my rollicking misadventure in the online world. The deeper I looked at the Internet—where, after all, I thrived professionally as the art critic for Slate.com and as the weekly television critic and then cultural blogger for the *New Republic Online*—the broader and more complex the social and cultural issues raised by it seemed. What was at stake was a question not of "media" but of who all of us were becoming in this new technological context. It was as much a question of investigating the influences on the Web as of thinking about the Web's influences on us. Goethe once said that the human condition never changes, but that throughout history, different aspects of being human present themselves or recede. Technology is a catalyst for bringing forth some human traits and suppressing others.

All the consciousness-shaping mass technologies of modern life provoked lively, impassioned arguments about what types of values they encourage and instill. Streams of polemical articles, essays, and books and numerous contentious conferences and public discussions had the effect of improving the quality of radio, television, and film—even as commercial pressures and incentives have intensified their shortcomings. The Internet has penetrated our lives more deeply than any other medium; it has far surpassed even television in its intimacy and immediacy. It deserves to be challenged by the same fundamental questions once posed to other revolutionary media.

This book tries to ask those questions. What interests are being served by the Internet? What values shaped it? What sorts of people dominate it? How is it affecting culture and social life? How is culture influencing the Internet? How are people learning to present themselves online? How are they learning to relate to other people online? What is the psychological and emotional and social cost of high-tech solitude? Are new voices being empowered, or are truly dissenting voices being drowned out in the name of free speech? Is democracy being served? Or are democratic values being perverted by the abuse of democratic principles?

The Internet is now a permanent part of our civilization. We can either passively allow it to obstruct our lives or guide it toward the fulfillment of its human promise. The choice is ours. Things really don't have to be the way they are.

PART ONE

"The World Is All That Is the Case"

I GO TO STARBUCKS, sit down, open my laptop, and turn it on. In the old days—ten years ago—I would be sitting with a pen and notebook, partly concentrating on my writing and partly aware of the people in the room around me. Back in that prehistoric time, my attention faced outward. I might see someone I know, or someone I'd like to know. I might passively enjoy trying to figure out why that couple in the middle of the room are speaking so intensely—are they moving closer together to relish their intimacy or because there is a crisis in their intimacy? And who is that guy with the fedora—and why the red sneakers? Is he an original, or the copy of an original? I might be watching everyone, but some people might be watching me, too. My situation is just as permeable as theirs. A stranger could come over to my table at any minute, his sudden physical presence before me unexpected, incalculable, absolutely enigmatic in the seconds before he becomes one kind of situation or another.

But here I am, sitting in the future—I mean the present—in front of my laptop. Just about everyone around me has a laptop open also. The small mass of barely variegated gray panels looks like a scene out of Fritz Lang's *Metropolis,* but with modems and Danishes. I can hardly see anyone else's face behind the screens, and no one seems to be doing anything socially or psychologically that might be fun to try to figure out. They are bent into their screens and toward their self-interest. My attention, too, is turned toward my ego. But I am paying attention in a different way from what I do when I read a book or a newspaper. I am opening e-mail sent to me, writing e-mail expressing one or another desire that belongs to me, clicking on Google looking for information to be used by me. Ten years ago, the space in a coffeehouse abounded in experience. Now that social space has been contracted into isolated points of wanting, all locked into separate phases of inwardness.

The new situation doesn't represent the "lack of community" suddenly produced by the Internet. That is the hackneyed complaint made, again and again, by people who don't seem to have thought through the unlovely aspects of "community"—its smug provincialism and punitive conventionalism, its stasis and xenophobia—which was in any case jeopardized and transformed by the advent of modernity two hundred years ago. The simple fact is that sometimes you don't want the quiet conformities induced by "community"; sometimes you simply want to be alone, yet together with other people at the same time. The old-fashioned café provided a way to both share and abandon solitude, a fluid, intermediary experience that humans are always trying to create and perfect. The Internet could have been its fulfillment. But sitting absorbed in your screenworld is a whole other story. You are socially and psychologically cut off from your fellow caffeine addicts, but mentally beset by e-mails, commercial "pop-ups," and a million temptations that may enchant in the moment—aimed as they are at your specific and immediate interests and desires—but in retrospect are time-wasting ephemera. It's not community that the laptopization of the coffeehouse has dispelled. It's the concrete, undeniable, immutable fact of our being in the world.

Before our screens, experience is collapsed into gratifying our desires on the one hand, and on the other either satisfying or refusing to satisfy the soliciting desires of other people—or entities. As the Viennese philosopher Ludwig Wittgenstein famously said, "The world is all that is the case." We have been flung into the world whether we like it or not. But the Internet creates a vast illusion that the physical, social world of interacting minds and hearts does not exist. In this new situation, the screen is all that is the case, along with the illusion that the screen projects of a world tamed, digested, abbreviated, rationalized, and ordered into a trillion connected units, called sites. This new world turns the most consequential fact of human life—other people—into seemingly manipulable half presences wholly available to our fantasies. It's a world controlled by our wrist and finger.

Yet the untamed, undigested, unrationalized, uncontrolled world is still there. People as thinking, feeling beings still exist. What form, then, do we take, in a world where there is—how else can I put it?—no world at all? To put it another way: What kind of idea do we have of the world when, day after day, we sit in front of our screens and enter further and further into the illusion that we ourselves are actually creating our own external reality out of our own internal desires? We become impatient with realities that don't gratify our impulses or satisfy our picture of reality. We find it harder to accept the immutable limitations imposed by identity, talent, personality. We start to behave in public as if we were acting in private, and we begin to fill our private world with gargantuan public appetites. In other words, we find it hard to bear simply being human.

This situation is not a crisis of technology. Rather, it is a social development that has been embodied in the new technology of the Internet, but not created by the Internet. The sudden onset of Web culture is really a dramatic turn in the timeless question of what it means to be a human being. What a shame that transformative new technologies usually either inspire uncritical celebration or incite bouts of nostalgia for a prelapsarian age that existed before said technology—anything for an uprising against cellphones and a return to the glorious phone booths of yore! The advent of new technologies pretty quickly becomes a pitched battle between the apostles of edge and Luddites wielding alarmist sentiments like pitchforks. Because each side is a caricature of itself, no one takes what is at stake very seriously at all.

And they are caricatures, for anyone who thinks technological innovation is bad in and of itself is an unimaginative crank. (I would rather go live on Pluto than return to the days of the phone booth and the desperate search for change.) But anyone who denies that technology has the potential to damage us if it is not put to good use is either cunning or naive. In the case of the Internet, the question is whether we let this remarkably promising opportunity—which, as we'll see, has until now largely been developed in service to commerce and capital—

shape us to its needs or put it in the service of our own. Do we keep acquiescing in the myopic glibness and carelessness that characterize how so many of us are using the Internet? Do we keep surrendering to the highly purposeful way vested interests are foisting it upon us?

COMFORTABLE UPHEAVAL

The future, we were once told, shocked. Well, the future is here. But no one is shocked.

The sensational evidence of upheaval is everywhere. You can read about it in the newspaper or see it on the news by the hour. A lonely middle-aged carpenter in Arizona meets a Brazilian woman online, visits her in Rio de Janeiro twice, and then, on his third encounter with her, is murdered by his new girlfriend, her real boyfriend, and a hired assassin. A sting operation sweeps up hundreds of pedophiles luring their prey in Internet chat rooms. Computer hackers use the Internet to nearly bring down the government of Estonia. An anonymous Web site reveals the identities of federally protected witnesses in capital cases. Social-networking sites like MySpace and the video-blog site called YouTube turn the most graphic inhumanity—a Texas policeman puts up photos of a dismembered woman; anonymous users post footage of American soldiers in Iraq being gunned down—into numbing new forms of entertainment.

The Internet's most consequential changes in our lives, however, are the ones woven into our everyday routines. Maybe your teenage son—or daughter—spends hours every day and night corresponding with dozens of new "friends" on MySpace or Facebook; perhaps he's uploading a forty-minute-long video of himself dancing naked, alone in his room, onto YouTube, one of the world's most highly trafficked sites. Maybe your officemate is addicted to political blogs like Little Green Footballs, or Instapundit, or Firedoglake, in which dozens, sometimes hundreds, of people, argue with each other passionately, sometimes abusively, on interminable threads of commenters. Or your other officemate spends all of his time buying merchandise on eBay, or your boss, a high-powered attorney, closes her door on her lunch hour and logs on to JDate, a Jewish dating service, where she fields inquiries from dozens of men.

Perhaps your husband is, at this very moment, shut away in his office somewhere in your home, carrying on several torrid online affairs at the same time under his various aliases: "Caliente," "Curious," "ActionMan." When he emerges from his sequestered lair, red-faced and agitated, is it because he has been arguing for moderation with "KillBush46" on the political blog Daily Kos, has failed in his bid to purchase genuine military-issue infrared night goggles on eBay, or has been masturbating while instant-messaging "Prehistorica12"?

Then again, maybe your husband died four years ago from a rare disease, and thanks to information you discovered on the Web, you were able to find a drug that kept him alive for twice as long as he would have lived without it. An Internet grief support group helped get you through the pain of your loss and introduced you to people who are now trusted friends. They led you, in turn, to an online dating service where you met your second husband, and began a new life.

Like all significant technologies, the Internet is a blessing and a curse. Or, rather, it is obviously a blessing and obscurely a curse. It would be tedious to recite the Internet's wonders as a tool for research and a medium for connectivity in detail here—in any case, those wonders have been touted far and wide for the last decade by an all-too-willing media. But the transformations are real. For the first time in human history, a person can have romance, friendship, and sex (sort of); be fed, clothed, and entertained; receive medical, legal, and just about every other type of advice; collect all sorts of information, from historical facts to secrets about other people—all without leaving home. For the first time in human history, a technology exists that allows a person to lead as many secret lives, under a pseudonym, as he is able to manage. For the first time in human history, a person can broadcast his opinions, beliefs, and most intimate thoughts—not to mention his face, or any other part of his body—to tens of millions of other people.

The simple fact is that more and more people are able to live in a more comfortable and complete self-enclosure than ever before.

THE BIG LIE

Since the rise of the Internet just ten years ago, the often irrational boosterism behind it has been for the most part met by criticism that is timid, defensive, and unfocused. The Internet is possibly the most radical transformation of private and public life in the history of humankind, but from the way it is publicly discussed, you would think that this gigantic jolt to the status quo had all the consequences of buying a new car. "The Internet," the *New York Times* casually reports, represents "a revolution in politics and human consciousness." Online sex is "changing the lives of billions" in Asia, writes *Time* magazine with a shrug, and follows that astounding headline with what amounts to a lifestyle article ("A continent of 3 billion human beings is getting sexy and kicking the guilt . . . say a sincere hosanna to the Internet, which not only allows wired Asians to hook up but also to find out about whatever may titillate or tantalize them"). Everyone agrees the Internet has the same "epochal" significance that the printing press once did. But after the printing press made its appearance in Europe, three hundred years had to go by before the "revolutionary" new invention began to seep down from the scholar's cloister into everyday life. Even the telephone and television, the most transformative technologies of modern times, took decades to reshape "human consciousness," to borrow the *Times*'s grandiose tone. The Internet has radically changed almost every level of human experience, throughout most of the world, in just a few years. So why can't people be honest about the downside as well as the upside of what's happening to us?

Of course no one wants to stand athwart the future shaking a finger, mocking and scowling and scolding. No one wants to be a wet blanket at the party. Americans don't like naysayers, and we don't like backward lookers. Ours has got to be the only culture in the world where saying that someone belongs to "history" is a fatal insult. So what you usually get by way of criticism are sunny, facile, corporate-funded gestures toward criticism. A typical example is the Pew Internet & American Life Project. Its September 2006 report on the current state and future of Internet culture has been widely used by anxious or self-interested journalists to forecast, among other things, the death of newspapers and print magazines. According to the Pew Project, "Internet users have become more likely to note big improvements in their ability to shop and the way they pursue their hobbies and interests. A majority of internet users also consistently report that the internet helps them to do their job and improves the way they get information about health care." Pew also notes "addiction problems" for many Web visitors, but quickly concludes that for many respondents to the survey, " 'addiction' is an inappropriate notion to attach to people's interest in virtual environments." The report then adds this creepy glance into the future: "Tech 'refuseniks' will emerge as a cultural group characterized by their choice to live off the network. Some will do this as a benign way to limit information overload, while others will commit acts of violence and terror against technology-inspired change."

Maybe one reason why the Pew report is so upbeat about its subject is that eight of the twelve people who wrote it have a financial or professional stake in the Internet. For them, any opposition to the Internet's darker effects is resistance to "technology-inspired change" rather than skepticism that embraces technology but recoils at some of its effects. Naturally, in their eyes, much of the opposition could not possibly be rational. It would have to come in the form of "violence and terror."

Along with Web boosters like the authors of the Pew study, who are motivated by material self-interest, is another type of potent promoter: the utopian technophile. We will meet several different varieties of these along our way. One of the most energetic and persuasive is Kevin Kelly, Internet guru, co-founder of *Wired* magazine, and the author of two hugely influential books on Internet culture—*Out of Control: The New Biology of*

Machines, Social Systems, and the Economic World and *New Rules for the New Economy: 10 Radical Strategies for a Connected World.* While the Pew report covered general patterns of usage, Kelly has a vision of social and cultural transformation:

> What will entertainment technology look like in 20 years? Let's listen to what technology says. First, technology has no preference between real and simulations—(so) neither will our stories. The current distinction between biological actors and virtual actors will cease, just as the distinction between real locations and virtual locations has almost gone. The choice will simply come down to what is less expensive. The blur between real and simulated will continue to blur the line between documentary and fiction. As straight documentaries continue to surge in popularity in the next 20 years, so will hybrids between fiction and nonfiction. We'll see more reality shows that are scripted, scripted shows that run out of control, documentaries that use actors, actors that are robotic creations, news that is staged, stories that become news and the total collision and marriage between fantasy and the found.

Now, Kelly may well be right. Yet in his feverish devotion to "technology," he sees nothing wrong with fake documentaries, deceitful "reality" shows, and "news that is staged." If technology decides that truth and falsehood shall be blurred, then for Kelly their "total collision and marriage"—whatever that means, exactly—is as historically determined, inevitable, and necessary as the Marxist belief in the dictatorship of the proletariat.

Despite the fact that Kelly cheerily predicts the imminent extinction of "old" media, nearly the entire journalistic establishment has embraced, in various degrees, his exuberant view of a dystopic future. For it is dystopic. What sane person wants a culture in which the border between truthfulness and lying is constantly being eroded? Nothing affects our values and perceptions, our thoughts and feelings, like the shows we watch, the movies we see, the books we read—and we watch far more than we read; Americans spend a large amount, if not a majority, of their leisure time being entertained. Kelly sees the engine of the Internet driving these cataclysmic changes in the culture. But journalists and other commentators are so afraid of appearing behind the times, or of being left behind, that the role the Internet plays in the disappearing borders of truth rarely gets talked about in public.

We know where we stand on a politician's lies; we know how to respond when we feel, for example, that the government's deceptions and lies led us into the Iraq war. But no one is making a cogent connection between the rise of the Internet and the accelerating blur of truth and falsity in culture—even though culture's subtle effects on our minds are a lot more profound in the long run than a politician's lies, which usually get discovered and exposed sooner or later. Instead of crying out against the manipulation of truth by "entertainment technology," as Kelly chillingly calls what used to be described as "having fun," we watch the general mendacity get turned into a joke—the comedian Stephen Colbert's celebrated quip about "truthiness"—and turn back to our various screens with a laugh.

People like the Pew group and Kevin Kelly are in a mad rush

to earn profits or to push a fervent idealism. But in their blink-ered eagerness to sell their outlooks—to focus our attention on what they are selling as an inevitable future—they rush right past the most obvious questions: How will the Internet affect the boundaries between people? As "information" consists more and more of reports from people's psyches, how will we be able to express intimate thoughts and feelings without sounding hackneyed and banal? As increasing numbers of people become dependent on the Internet, and the Internet is driven more and more by commerce—the sensational stock prices and sales of Google, MySpace, and YouTube, for example—how do we keep an obsession with the bottom line from overwhelming our lives? How do we carve out a space for a life apart from the Internet, and apart from economics?

UPGRADE AND BE HAPPY

Anyway, who wants to glower at the Internet when it brings such a cornucopia of wonders? Bill Gates describes what he considers the full potential of the Internet's developments:

> They will enable equal access to information and instanta-neous communication with anyone in the world. They will open up vast markets and opportunities to businesses of any size. They will transcend national borders, making possible a frictionless global economy. They will allow workers to be even more efficient and productive, and will have the potential to make jobs more stimulating and ful-filling. They will give developing nations the ability to

leapfrog the industrial era and move straight into the information age. They will help people and businesses in countries with large, dispersed populations to stay in touch, and help the smallest nations participate as equals in the global economy.

Gates says he is not blind to the Internet's pitfalls, either:

As more and more people store personal information on the Internet, how will we ensure that information is kept secure? As our economy becomes more dependent on bits than on atoms, how will we protect these resources from being damaged or devalued by hackers? As the barriers to information come down, how will we protect our children from negative and predatory influences? And as the Internet dissolves national borders, how will we help indigenous cultures coexist with an increasingly homogenous global culture?

Gates's radiant view of the future and his predictions of the problems that might obstruct the Internet's promise are reiterated throughout the media. They are the standard description of the Internet's bright side and its dark side. But there is something dark about Gates's sunniness; there is something rosy about his premonition of difficulties along the way. Consider the bad news first. Are the problems Gates foresees really problems at all? They have a red-herringish quality about them; they are by no means insoluble. Indeed, Gates frames these dilemmas produced by new technology in such a way that their resolution lies exclusively in the invention of newer technology.

For the way to keep information secure is to develop software that will do so. We can protect against hackers by constructing systems that thwart them. Advanced computer programs will shield our children from the dangers unleashed as "the barriers to information come down." (Notice how Gates makes even sexual predators seem like the necessary consequence of an unmitigated good: How could more information ever be anything but a marvelous beneficence? And who would use "negative and predatory influences" on children as an argument against opening the floodgates of information?)

As for the disruptions that the Internet might bring to impoverished, illiterate populations, Gates formulates this conflict as a cultural, not a social, clash. The answer, he implies, is simply to introduce the "indigenous" cultures to the techniques that are making the world "increasingly homogenous." Rather than honestly face the strange new perils the Internet has created, Gates's "realism" strengthens the impression of the Internet's power, permanence, and necessity. For Gates, the only answer to the Internet's dark side is the Internet itself.

One of the striking characteristics of conversation about the Internet is this circular, hermetic quality. The "key words and phrases," as the search engines like to say, in Gates's rosy picture of the future give you a sense of how he would answer the dilemmas posed by new technology: "access," "markets," "businesses," "economy," "efficient," "productive," "leapfrog the industrial era." Gates doesn't worry that the Internet will upset deep, irrational human needs and desires. For him, deep, irrational human needs and desires don't exist outside the super-rationally ordered universe of the Internet. And since economics is the simplest means of rationalizing human life,

Gates believes that being human can be defined strictly in economic terms.

Microsoft, however, had a long arrival. Over thirty years ago, in *The Coming of Post-Industrial Society*, the sociologist Daniel Bell predicted Bill Gates. Decades before Gates made the computer the means of assimilating human existence to an economic model, Bell saw how the computer would eventually embed everyday life in an economic framework.

2

Bait and Switch

THE FUTURE, DANIEL BELL wrote in the early 1970s, would be characterized by the application of what he called "intellectual technology." Bell defined this new technology as "the substitution of algorithms (problem-solving rules) for intuitive judgments." Life will be rationalized to such a degree that unpredictability will barely exist.

Now, these rational solutions—these "algorithms"—for life's irrational problems don't come from nowhere. According to Bell, they are derived from game and decision theory. These theories are modes of problem solving that apply mathematical equations to everyday life, and they are most frequently used in the area of economics. The rise of computers, Bell predicted in 1976, would make such methods of analysis widespread. Bell believed that an economic view of life was the core of a computer-centered culture.

This is precisely the dynamic that drives Gates's vision of the Internet. When Microsoft's founder speaks of a "frictionless" global economy, he isn't just conjuring up a world in which borders, tariffs, and protectionist restrictions no longer apply to streams of information borne instantaneously through virtual space. In Gates's personal idiom, "frictionless" seems to be an ideal that goes beyond the simple idea of increased efficiency. The odd term seems to reflect a desire to burst through the obstacles of space and time and a yearning to erase the chronic dilemmas that are the consequence of having a heart and a mind. This kind of evangelism invokes a new vision of utopia, a world where the enigmas of being human are solved, through the giant dazzling tool of the Internet, in the same way that economic problems are solved.

Which is why the Internet's most important boosters almost always end up speaking about the Internet in the language of economics. For all their visionary-like rhetoric about radically overhauling consciousness and culture, the revolution that they are really describing is the overthrow of disinterested existence by the ethos and priorities of business. Gates speaks primarily of markets and businesses. Kevin Kelly's two most influential "futuristic" books, as some people refer to them, both concern themselves with the Internet's relationship to business and the economy. Not for nothing did Kelly team up in the early 1990s with George Gilder, the right-wing ideologue, to work out in the pages of *Wired* a synthesis between "digital networks" and the free market.

The Internet's assimilation to a familiar economic idiom is why its more disorienting and destructive side has been so obscured. We use economic language—the ordinary language of buying and selling—every day. So when people like Gates and Kelly talk about the new medium almost exclusively in economic terms, even its most extreme aspects seem pedestrian. They seem like mere extensions of dilemmas that we have been facing for a long time. The *New York Times* article suggesting that the Internet might be a "revolution in politics and human consciousness" mundanely concludes that, contrary to the romantic expectations of some of its early theorists, cyberspace is "not really a different realm from the hard-wired world of ordinary experience, but would become an extension of it: a place where banking, shopping, conversation and business transactions could take place." The *Time* magazine effusion about online sex segues into a discussion of the profits reaped by Asian Web sites devoted to sex.

Even religious authorities, who you assume would be sensitive to the Internet's effects on mores, attention span, vulnerability to addiction, and other issues, tame it in cost-benefit terms. A Florida newspaper speaks of the spectacularly popular minister Rick Warren's "lifelong fascination with the evangelistic possibilities of technology and the first test pilots of his belief that the Internet is, like the printing press, an epochal invention that will multiply the message of Christ and transform the future church. 'Every time God's word is put in a new technology, there's a spiritual awakening.' " In other words, the Internet will add millions of people to Warren's congregation.

This dominance of the idiom of exchange extends beyond the language we use to talk about the Internet. The same idiom defines the experience of using the Web. The most vivid examples of how commerce has normalized shocking change is the way the Web has routinized forbidden sexual appetites and images. I type "masochism.com" into my browser, and sure enough, my computer promptly brings me to a site called fetishplanet, which offers a menu listing links like "Pure Smut," "Gyno Shots," and "Gangbang." I guess the masochism was just a tease. Photographs of various sexual configurations adorn the menu's borders: a woman performing oral sex on an enormous phallus; a woman being penetrated from behind; a topless woman baring her breast and displaying what seems to be her penis (under the category "Sluts with Nuts"). What's extraordinary isn't the dirty pictures. Pornography has been around since the dawn of history. What's remarkable is the way these scenes of graphic sex have been assimilated to the routine conventions of economic transaction.

I click on a category and the next screen offers a free "trailer" for me to view, and then invites me to "join now." Several options present themselves. I can choose a "7 Days Trial," "3 Days Trial," "30 Days Full," or "90 Days Full." Fetishplanet also is pleased to tell me that it will accept my credit card, and if I don't have a credit card ("No Credit Card, No Problem!"), it will gladly take an online check or sign me up over the phone. I'm also informed that this "Is an AOL Friendly Website and Works on All Browsers." The assimilation of taboo images to the everyday language of doing business produces a strange effect. It domesticates the taboo while at the same time making the everyday transactional world more porous, more open to the forbidden. The wolf of unbridled appetite slips into everyday convention in the sheep's clothing of commercial language.

What's more, your immersion in this online world of forbidden images takes place on your home computer, where you pay your bills, correspond with friends, search for ordinary information, buy a plane ticket, or reserve a table at a restaurant.

Everything, taboo and familiar, occurs on the same screen. The border between private desire and public behavior begins to slip and slide. Clothed in mundane convention, the shock of taboo feels like the rerun of a sitcom. Couched in the rational and rationalizing language of business, the displacements, distortions, and disorientations of the Web go unseen and unexamined.

This nice coffee-like blending of the forbidden and the familiar is the brainchild of the "new entrepreneurs" who have successfully peddled the idea that the market happily accommodates all human values, from the most "cultural" and creative to the most private and antisocial. Taking a cue from the frictionless vision and commerce-saturated language of Web culture, they describe a world where business values define all of our options.

THE MYTH OF THE "BOURGEOIS BOHEMIAN"

Web culture is the final stage in the long, slow assimilation of subversive values to conventional society. With the advent of the Internet, business culture has now strangely become identified with untrammeled mental and spiritual freedom—a freedom once defined by its independence from the commercial realm.

The lineage of this idea about conventional society's absorption of subversive notions goes back a long way. Karl Marx scathingly attributed a dynamic to capitalism that later thinkers celebrated as the spirit of artistic modernism: "All that is solid melts into air." The American economist Joseph Schumpeter spoke, with a sober realization of the human toll involved, of business's "creative-destructive" energies. In the 1950s, Lionel Trilling wrote with an air of disapproval about the seeming absorption of avant-garde and "adversarial" values into the mainstream (he worried as much about the mainstream as about the fate of the avant-garde); and Irving Howe lamented the co-optation of independent intellectuals by government, academia, and commerce. Tom Wolfe got his start by mocking the slow diffusion of subversive aesthetic energies into conventional society; Tom Frank's *The Conquest of Cool* is the most recent updating of this idea. But for the many differences between them, all these figures agreed that creativity and iconoclasm were transformed in the hands of financiers and merchants. A vast gulf of meaning separated the assimilated from the assimilators.

In our time, that has changed. The critique of conventionalized subversion or iconoclasm has gone from indictment, to lament, to mockery, to the celebration of a new symbiosis. We have undergone a complete "transvaluation of values," the phrase that the German philosopher Friedrich Nietzsche used to describe the process by which a new way of looking at the world slips into our familiar outlook. Nietzsche believed that Christianity, for example, had "transvalued" earlier pagan and aristocratic values of heroism, power, and fame into meekness, humility, and eternal life. The early Christians did this while retaining pagan vocabulary, so that Jesus was still a "prince" and God as "mighty" as any Roman emperor; God's realm was as much a "kingdom" as that of Nero. But although the former vocabulary remained, the new values had an entirely different meaning.

Something very like Nietzsche's transvaluation of values has taken place in this country over the past ten years, simultaneous with the rise of the information age. It is now conventional wisdom that the business culture is as playful, creative, and benign as the adversarial/counter/bohemian—choose your terminology—culture that once excoriated the former as soulless, heartless, and devoid of playfulness and imagination. The language of making money has become identified with the language of iconoclastic creativity. As a result, Internet boosterism can conceal psychic displacement behind rhetoric about market opportunities. It can hide the commodifying of ideas and emotions behind hyperbole about liberating avenues of fantasy and play.

David Brooks's "Bobo"—short for "bourgeois bohemian"—was a very shrewd, perhaps even opportunistic crystallization of the Internet's transvaluation. Brooks's *Bobos in Paradise*, which appeared in 2000, helped legitimize the Internet's new atmosphere even as it eagerly rushed to conform to it.

Brooks is motivated by a simple idea. The new "renegade executives are both corporate and genuinely countercultural . . . educated folk who have one foot in the bohemian world of creativity and another foot in the bourgeois realm of ambition and worldly success. The members of the new information age elite are bourgeois bohemians . . . the bourgeoisie has, in fact, revived itself by absorbing (and being absorbed by) the energy of bohemianism." Brooks's book immediately became a best seller, and his concept of the "bourgeois bohemian" was celebrated as having captured the spirit of our time.

Bobos in Paradise teems with examples drawn from Silicon Valley and its offshoots. "One of the ironies of the age," writes Brooks, in a section headed "The Countercultural Capitalists," "is that the one realm of American life where the language of 1960s radicalism remains strong is the business world." He goes on to cite examples from Apple, Lucent Technologies, and *Wired* magazine and its "Silicon Valley advertisers who use the color schemes of 1968 Jefferson Airplane street posters." Brooks actually believes, on the evidence of mere appearances—as if hypocrisy did not exist!—that a businessman devoted to making money can at the same time be a person revolted by a life spent pursuing money.

Brooks rested his argument on the flimsiest of premises. The proof that business had become "bohemian," he declared, was that it had appropriated the rhetoric and style of bohemian-type people. Businessmen referred to Gandhi and Jack Kerouac and used words like "revolution" and "meaning." Entrepreneurs wore sandals to work and allowed their employees to dress in jeans, and some people even came into the office with "tousled hair." Brooks presents numerous examples: The "recruiting literature" at Hewlett-Packard reads, "At HP, people don't become cogs in some giant corporate machine. From their first day of work here, people are given important responsibilities and are encouraged to grow." "Pitney Bowes Credit Corporation has actually designed its offices in Connecticut to resemble a small village." "The hearing aid firm Oticon puts everybody's desk on wheels so they can be wheeled around the vast workspace." Wheee! "As Xerox's John Seely Brown told *Fortune*, 'The job of leadership today is not just to make money. It's to make meaning.'"

But just as the early Christians' use of "power," "kingdom," "prince," and "immortality" meant something very different from the meaning the Romans invested in these words, American businessmen who appropriated the language of "bohemia" were filling old bottles with new wine. You could even say that they were Romans borrowing Christian language in order to mask greed behind an idiom of decency and creativity.

Just a few years after Brooks published his book, Hewlett-Packard fired 14,500 employees—10 percent of its workforce. Its shareholders continued to collect huge dividends, and the company's executives still brought home hundreds of millions of dollars a year. Pitney Bowes, though flourishing, kicked 800 employees out of their nice little village. And despite doubling its profits, Xerox cut 3,500 jobs in 2005. Though raking it in, the company had failed to meet Wall Street expectations of accelerating growth. So much for making "meaning" instead of money. As for Oticon, what Brooks never tells you, and what the breathless boobies who extolled his Bobos didn't bother to find out, was that the company was Danish. For all its "bohemian" rhetoric and style, American business was still devoted to the grim bottom line.

Nevertheless, Brooks's thesis greatly appealed to its audience, whom Brooks anointed the new "information elite." He ended his book with a flattering tribute to his readers: "They have the ability to go down in history as the class that led America into another golden age." A new myth was born, one that identified the pursuit of profits with creative play and made profit a justification for just about any social or cultural activity. Months after Brooks published his book, Frank Rich wrote an article about the porn business for the *New York Times Magazine,* in which he enthused that the industry's earnings were so astronomical that "there may be no other product in the cultural marketplace that is more explicitly American." This shuffling of values had the effect of further establishing and legitimizing the Internet's totalizing economic framework.

Brooks's New Entrepreneur boasts that he has absorbed countercultural values to such an extent that he threatens the established order. He talks about overthrowing hierarchies, about expanding democracy, about making people both consumers and producers. He advocates a breaking down of mass culture into specialized niches that cater to individual taste. But rather than living proof of the symbiosis between counterculture and business culture, he is a striking example of the latter's capacity for driving a wedge between action and rhetoric. Today's New Entrepreneur represents an all-out assault on the idea that a person can exist outside the sphere of the marketplace.

This new type of businessman actually existed twenty years before Brooks published his book. He was born amid the throes of the Internet industry, and just as ordinary economic language now provides cover for Internet upheaval, futuristic rhetoric once concealed the bottom-line mentality that has driven the Internet from almost its inception.

Fred Turner's influential *From Counterculture to Cyberculture*, an attempt to make a positive connection between the Internet and 1960s counterculture, unwittingly demonstrate how Web culture definitively transvalued business and humanistic values. Turner's central figure is Stewart Brand, who began as a back-to-earth New Communalist in northern California's hippie culture forty years ago and eventually founded the *Whole Earth Catalog,* a whimsical yet shrewdly profit-oriented guide to countercultural products and services.

Brand had discovered computers at Stanford University in the early 1960s. Unlike some of his fellow communalists, though, he didn't see cybernetics (or technology in general) as a plague on the human spirit. He would not have agreed with another countercultural figure at the time, a very young Robert Stone—who later became a celebrated novelist—that the landing on the moon represented an "industrialization" of that heretofore romantic orb. No, Brand admirably envisioned computers as a potent instrument in the creation of an egalitarian, antihierarchical society. As communication and the spread of information became more and more widespread, social and political barriers would fall one by one. This is what Brand declared he believed.

From Counterculture to Cyberculture is representative of the kind of reverent, kid-glove commentary and coverage the Internet has gotten since it began to overwhelm the culture in the 1990s. On the one hand, Turner is too smart not to see a transvaluation of values where he hoped to find genuine consistency. Following Brand along the route of his evolution from "itinerant photographer" in the mid-1960s to economic libertarian and friend of George Gilder, Turner presents the portrait of an exceedingly shrewd man, indifferent to the very social ideals he once claimed to espouse. Even as Brand was speaking of "personalization" and "decentralization," he was co-founding the Global Business Network, whose high-paying clients included oil companies, military contractors, and the Department of Defense.

How far has Brand come from his so-called hippie days? Writing in the *New Yorker* about the vast urban squalor in Lagos, Nigeria, George Packer sees mostly generations of people mired in hopeless immobility. Then he quotes Stewart Brand, now a "business strategist," who works in California:

> "Squatter cities are vibrant," [Brand] writes in a recent article on mega cities. "Each narrow street is one long bustling market." He sees in the explosive growth of "aspirational shantytowns" a cure for Third World poverty and an extraordinary profit-making opportunity. "How does all this relate to businesspeople in the developed world?" Brand asks. "One-fourth of humanity trying new things in new cities is a lot of potential customers, collaborators, and competitors."

"In the dirty gray light of Lagos," Packer writes disgustedly, "Brand's vision of a global city of interconnected entrepreneurs seems perverse." However, despite his conscientious notations on the type of shifting sentiments Packer exposes in Brand, Turner refuses to be discouraged in his quest for a warm and snuggly Internet. Like so many people who write about technology in America, Turner seems to harbor a terror of being perceived as a naysayer who has fallen behind the times. He observes that for Brand, "the rhetoric of community provided the ideological cover necessary to transform a potentially stark and single-minded market transaction into a complex, multidimensional act." That is to say, Brand is "talking the talk." Yet at the same time, Turner insists that Brand's entrepreneurial activities "served as a way to preserve the social ideals of the New

Communalist movement in the face of rapid technological and social change." But how can mere "rhetoric of community" serving as "ideological cover" transform a transaction into anything that is not, essentially, a transaction? Like David Brooks, Turner believes in mere appearances the way devoutly religious people believe in God. For him, the business culture's absorption of subversive values is both a matter of faith and an unambiguous moral and intellectual success.

DOING GOOD vs. DOING WELL

Interestingly, the "complex, multidimensional act" that Turner refers to is one of the most consequential occasions in the history of the Internet. In 1985, Stewart Brand invented a computerized conferencing system associated with the *Whole Earth Catalog*. He called it the WELL, which was short for "Whole Earth 'Lectronic Link." The WELL was the first and most influential online community, a true forerunner of the millions of Web sites and chat rooms that populate the Web today. Turner explains precisely in what sense the WELL was complex and multidimensional:

> On the WELL, the boundary between public and private was extraordinarily fluid. As a result, any given contribution to a WELL conference might have value simultaneously in multiple domains—collective, interpersonal, and economic . . . the system offered access to information and expertise that could be transformed into income elsewhere.

Turner calls this an "economic heterarchy," which he defines like this: "Hierarchies create wealth by inviting more than one way of evaluating worth." In plain English, this means that the WELL's "users" became adept at converting their private thoughts into income-producing units of exchange. The WELL's inspiration was to turn leisure time—the sharing of personal experience—into work. As Cliff "Fig" Figallo, one of the WELL's founders, described the WELL's beginnings:

> At first, for me, I didn't understand the technology or the implications. Soon enough, though, I became aware . . . of the need to build and maintain relationships between people and to preserve the structure that supported those relationships. I also became aware, largely through Tex's [John Coate, another of the WELL's founders] dogged insistence, that those relationships were the only "product" we had to sell . . . The personalities stood out and the experience of participating mind-to-mind with people became compelling, fascinating, inspiring. We could feel the effects of our decisions on people's behavior and the immediate feedback, though sometimes jarring, was something we knew was unique in the business world.

It wasn't long before the most frequent and popular users became keenly aware of the WELL's aim of catching the commercial eye. (The small online company was eventually sold to Salon.com.) Indeed, many of them were freelance writers and professional journalists fishing for copy. So other members of the WELL customized themselves to appeal to the journalists—a story in a newspaper or national magazine meant more publicity, and thus more profits for the WELL's proprietors. On the WELL, behind every intimate expression lay a self-advertisement; hidden in the invitation to a relationship was the bid for a profitable "connection." As Katie Hafner, a *New York Times* technology reporter, writes, in *The Well: A Story of Love, Death and Real Life in the Seminal Online Community*: "If the ability to project an engaging personality through the filter of flat ASCII text was a talent few people truly possessed, it was clear that there were plenty of people who wanted to try." The WELLians were learning how to turn their private experience into a public commodity.

For the pioneering WELL was all about packaging people, or helping people to package themselves. Brand and his partners developed "conference" sites with names like "Mind," "Sexuality," and "True Confessions." Inevitably, the people who participated in these prototypes of today's chat rooms strived to make themselves sound as intellectual, sexual, and confessional as they could. They were learning to do what by now comes naturally to everybody who pays or plays on the Internet today. They were learning how to perform their privacy. And when Brand and his partners thought that the electronic conversation lacked excitement, they simply posted provocative entries to mix things up and keep the subscribers' money coming in.

For all their stated commitment to the online community's privacy, decency, and integrity, the WELL's owners never failed to put people last. Consider the case of Tom Mandel and Maria Syndicus. Mandel, one of Brand's colleagues at the Global Business Network, met Syndicus online at the WELL and the two of them proceeded to have an affair. They soon announced their engagement on the WELL. But shortly after that, Syndicus fell ill with cancer and Mandel abruptly withdrew from her. Wounded by his behavior, Syndicus privately broke off the engagement. She then took up with another man, whom she also had met on the WELL. Mandel retaliated. Ensconced alone before his computer, Mandel began persecuting Syndicus online, stalking her at online conferences and posting venomous comments attacking her. Finally, he found a way to delete all of Syndicus's posts as soon as she made them.

You would think that Brand, devoted as he claimed to be to the countercultural ideals of wholesome community and individual decency, would have immediately expelled Mandel from the WELL. That's not what happened. After being told by Brand to stay off the WELL for a few days, Mandel was allowed to return. WELL members were stunned. They shouldn't have been. As Hafner writes in her mostly worshipful account, "For years, Mandel had generated not just words, but controversy, which generated business. He literally provoked people to participate." It makes you wonder whether Mandel's sensationally dramatic meltdown with Syndicus was a real crisis at all. As Hafner says about the episode, "Mandel's erratic behavior attracted members of the WELL's community like bloodhounds to the scent. They tracked each turn of events avidly, feeding on the few known facts that could be summarized in bullets." Eventually, *Time* magazine hired Mandel to advise it on its own online forum, run by AOL—"because," Hafner writes, "if anyone knew how to keep a discussion going, he did."

Mandel, who died in 1995, had mastered the art of packaging his interiority, an innovation that would become the driving engine behind Web culture. The counterculture had sought to practice the idea that creative personal expression was the essence of an authentic existence. The WELL, drawing strength from the Internet culture's belief that the market contains all values, put personal expression up for sale. Now our interior lives could be sold like merchandise, and all under cover of the Bobo's seemingly outlaw energy.

3

The Me Is the Message

YOUTUBE IS THE NAME of a Web site that allows people to post any type of video they want, and lonelygirl15 is the name of a YouTube user who is obviously a contemporary master of self-packaging. On her videoblog, she presented herself as a six-teen-year-old girl named Bree and purported to tell the true story of her life as a sheltered adolescent who is homeschooled by her strict, religious father and mother. Bree's parents belong to a sinister and secretive cult known as "The Order," and the drama of Bree's story revolved around her attempts to free her-self and her family from the cult's repressive leaders.

As the domestic suspense mounted—and as Bree slipped into her episodic tale more and more names of popular YouTube bloggers—lonelygirl15 began to draw increasing at-tention. But despite the fact that she even had her own page on MySpace, a Web site where anyone can start a blog and share personal information with other people, lonelygirl15 raised doubts about her authenticity. Before long, other bloggers and finally the mainstream media exposed her saga as a hoax. Bree was actually an aspiring young actress named Jessica Rose, an American living in New Zealand, who was abetted in her elaborate fraud by two filmmakers. Not only that, but Rose was also being advised by the Creative Artists Agency, perhaps the world's most powerful theatrical agency, based in Beverly Hills.

By the time the lonelygirl hoax was revealed, the country had long been reeling from a series of public betrayals. Enron officials had lied to their shareholders. A *New York Times* reporter named Jayson Blair had lied to his editors. James Frey had fabricated events in his best-selling, Oprah-endorsed memoir. Most consequentially, and outrageously, of all, President Bush had clearly lied to America and to the world about the existence of weapons of mass destruction in Iraq, and also about a connection between Saddam Hussein and Al Qaeda. You might have expected an exasperated American public, or at least the American media and blogosphere, to be equally angered by the revelation that YouTube and MySpace had been infiltrated by dishonest and powerful vested interests.

Instead, lonelygirl15, who was very much the product of an old public-relations paradigm, became even more popular in certain circles. So much so that Virginia Heffernan—a *New York Times* television critic and one of the mainstream journalists who uncovered the fraud—began to comment on lonelygirl15's ongoing story as though it were a legitimate work of popular entertainment. And so it has become. Jessica Rose herself appeared on the cover of *Wired* magazine not long after she was exposed as a fake. In 2006, the United Nations hired her to make an antipoverty video. In the film, she sits in front of a camera alone in her bedroom as lonelygirl15 and speaks, as they say, truth to power.

Once upon a time, a fraud like Rose's, subsidized and orchestrated by a powerful and ruthless corporate patron, would not even have made it into the public eye, and if by chance it had, the dishonest stunt would have aroused much mockery and disgust. Back then, people enjoyed being enchanted by art's illusions, but they didn't like being deceived by the misrepresentation of facts. But once upon a time, the public had not become accustomed to seeing and hearing private life enacted as though it were a fabricated performance. Not long ago, in the burgeoning age of confessionalism, private life was being made public all over the place, but it was still considered authentic private experience. Now we have the widespread practice of what you might call "The Genuine Hoax."

Almost thirty years ago, in *The Culture of Narcissism*, Christopher Lasch noted a swelling tide of "confessional" writing in which "many writers now rely on mere self-disclosure to keep the reader interested, appealing not to his understanding but to his salacious curiosity about the private lives of famous people." Though Lasch admired much contemporary memoir for its ability "to achieve a critical distance from the self and gain insight," he decried the tendency of many of its authors to use the form "as a means of deflecting criticism and disclaiming responsibility for [their] actions."

Lasch believed that all this evasive self-obsession was the result of a narcissistic culture that had two simultaneous effects. It drove people further into themselves, and it created an inner emptiness by exalting the self and cutting it off from reality.

Such isolated self-scrutiny, packed with psychiatric clichés, made people so self-conscious that they felt as though they were performing their existence rather than living it. Modern art's habit of mixing art and life, especially in the street theater of the 1960s, heightened what Lasch called the "theatrics of everyday life." The dangerous result, as Lasch saw it, was a feeling of general unreality, about oneself and about one's environment.

Lasch's groundbreaking book was prescient in many respects, especially in its definition of the narcissist as someone "whose sense of self depends on the validation of others whom he nevertheless degrades"—a characteristic that, as we shall see, animates the blogosphere. Yet for all his criticism of empty self-absorption, and of the deleterious effects of an artistic blurring of reality's boundaries, Lasch never questioned memoirists' claim to be telling the truth about their lives. Nor did he ever question the veracity of the performing individual's self-conscious performances. For Lasch, the utter banality, as well as the lack of self-knowledge, that lay behind these self-disclosures and self-dramatizations was what he found so culturally and humanly disheartening.

What Lasch could not have foreseen was the effect commerce and the technology of the Internet would have on the way people present their inner lives in public. The 1960s may have accelerated the collapse of the private realm into the public realm; that era of self-expression and shifting boundaries in all areas of life may have famously made the personal the political. But the Internet's vision of "consumers" as "producers" has turned inner life into an advanced type of commodity.

People don't want their privacy invaded. They now want other people, as many people as possible, to watch them as they carefully craft their privacy into a marketable, public style. Real private life has gone underground; it is a type of contraband. Real, uncalculated, uncustomized, untailored outbursts of what has been buried in inner life become publicly laughed at and mocked. Think of Howard Dean's scream, or of Bill Clinton's flash of temper on television when an interviewer implied that the former president's lack of vigilance led to the attacks on September 11 (as scripted as that bit of unscripted-seeming drama might have been), or of just about any of the gaffes made by public figures that are expertly snagged and derided by co-medians like Jon Stewart and Stephen Colbert and spread via YouTube and blogs.

The reason why lonelygirl15's hoax has been accepted, rather than stigmatized and rejected, is that people have now come to expect inner life to be performed, rather than disclosed. The truth or untruth of facts presented as facts in the course of a performance is never at issue. Ironically, however, many of the videoblogs and blogs that elevate the packaged private life are the very same ones that ruin anyone whose private thoughts slip through the public package.

THE MYTH OF "SELF-EXPRESSION"

Internet boosters love this aphorism by Marshall McLuhan: "The user is the content." Everyone agrees that McLuhan was stating what has come to be the fundamental principle of Internet culture: the audience determines the form and content of its medium; the consumer organizes and controls and—most important—generates his product. The culture becomes, to use another buzzword, "user-generated." Jon Pareles, the *New York Times*'s chief music critic, explains what user-generated media means:

> An ever-expanding heap of personal ads, random photos, private blathering, demo recordings and camcorder video clips . . . a flood of grainy TV excerpts, snarkily edited film clips, homemade video diaries, amateur music videos and shots of people singing along with their stereos . . . It's on Web sites like YouTube, MySpace, Dailymotion, PureVolume, GarageBand and Metacafe. It's homemade art independently distributed and inventively promoted. It's borrowed art that has been warped, wrecked, mocked and sometimes improved. It's blogs and open-source software and collaborative wikis and personal Web pages. It's word of mouth that can reach the entire world.

For Pareles, there's nothing new about this riot of self-produced activity. "I prefer something a little more old-fashioned" than the term "user-generated," he writes. "Self-expression."

But self-expression is not the same thing as imagination. "Self-expression" is one of those big, baggy terms bulging with lots of cultural change and cultural history to the point where it gestures toward a kind of general meaning without expressing a particular one. The phrase is a compound of American radical individualism, conventional go-get-'em entrepreneurial initiative, and countercultural "do-your-own-thing" idiosyncrasy. It can mean standing on the street and shouting "Fuck," playing a CD of your favorite band as loud as you can, finger painting, or taking funny pictures with the camera on your cellphone. If your four-month-old poops on a guest's lap, you might drily say that he is "expressing himself." And you would not be entirely ironic.

What "self-expression" does not mean is the making of art—of any kind of art, popular or high. You would not refer to *The Catcher in the Rye* as a major feat of self-expression, any more than you would call the latest album by the Flaming Lips the band's most interesting self-expression yet. We know instinctively, even if we can't put it into words, that art is a form of expression that mysteriously accommodates our experience without actually addressing our particular experience. It speaks to us even though it doesn't know we're there. Vermeer wasn't thinking of you or me when he painted *Girl with a Pearl Earring,* but the painting moves us nonetheless. And we know, in the depths of our response to the painting, that it couldn't touch us so deeply if it were merely an expression of the self that produced it. Rather, it expresses us. At the same time, it doesn't tell us anything revealing about Vermeer the person—any more than Salinger's novel or even a song by the Flaming Lips tells us anything specific about the artists who wrote the book and the music.

The comparison of art to self-expression would make no sense if the latter had not entirely supplanted the former in the lives of self-expression's vast number of producers and consumers. I click on to YouTube as I write this, and these are a few of the top-ten videoblogs: a young bald man with round, wire-framed glasses doing a rapidly spoken monologue about Valentine's Day (two days away); a video drama whose plot its creators tell us is " 'Real World' meets 'Justice League' when low-level superheroes trying to break into the big time all live in the same building"; a father, who is sitting in the front seat of his parked car, telling his young son, strapped into a car seat in the back, how to "pick up chicks"; a film of a goat giving birth ("yes, we really named the goat YouTube"); a "mash-up"—or re-edit—of a real Senate hearing with black singers playing Condoleezza Rice and Alan Keyes, who rap to the real-life senators. Some of this is fun, all of it is self-indulgent, none of it is the type of creative act that moves or touches me or even makes me laugh. For all the amusement I experience watching these little films, I feel bored and empty afterward.

Pareles would call these YouTube performances "self-expression." But this raises a question. What is the self being expressed? Like the novice performers on *American Idol,* every one of these videobloggers is performing some piece of popular culture; you recognize the shticks of a hundred comedians you've seen on television; "Real World" meets "Justice League" is exactly that; the rap style of "Condoleezza" and friends is about ten years old. All these mostly young people on this supposedly wild, egalitarian, hierarchy-shattering medium, where anything supposedly goes, are cautious and derivative. They are pitching themselves to an audience already familiar with their routines, which have been certified by popular culture as having been successful. What happened to all the "self-expression"?

Here's one explanation. As Pareles tells us in the beginning of his article, Rupert Murdoch recently paid $580 million for the "ever-expanding heap" of self-expression on MySpace, and Google bought YouTube's "flood of grainy TV excerpts" for $1.65 billion. Powerfully remunerative eyes have been on these so-called free spaces of self-expression since the beginning.

Before Vermeer, or J. D. Salinger, or even the Flaming Lips did their thing, they learned how to do it. The marketplace was not watching them as they learned. The majority of YouTubers, on the other hand, never took the time to patiently master a craft. They rush online and try to sell—for attention has become a new type of income—whatever is at hand: a hiccuping puppy or an invented memory. Doing their thing and doing business in the marketplace are the very same activity.

QUID PRO(SUMER) QUO

To really grasp the idea that "the user is the content," you have to understand the term "prosumer." The word was coined about thirty years ago by Alvin Toffler, one of a group of business gurus known as futurists. Futurology, in fact, shares its history with the Internet. Both have their origins in American military research during the first years of the Cold War. The Internet grew out of the Advanced Research Projects Agency, established by a NASA anxious to reclaim a technological edge over the Soviets after the Russians launched Sputnik in 1957. Futurology took off in the 1940s, sponsored by military think tanks devoted to "trend watching" and "scenario development." Since business is also interested in how future events might affect economic prospects, the futurists soon shifted from serving military interests to working for business ones.

And it wasn't long before the futurists stopped merely making predictions for business and started to predict trends that would reap large profits for business, and thus bring in more business for themselves. John Naisbitt's *Megatrends,* Herman Kahn's *The Coming Boom,* and, most sensationally, Toffler's *Future Shock* didn't just prognosticate the optimal conditions for business. These books presented the optimal conditions for business as the inevitable next stage of civilization. In this, the American futurists weirdly resembled the Russian Marxists, who also conceived of history as inevitably conforming to their idea of the future.

Though there were minor differences between them, the futurists all shared two goals. One was to predict the future in terms of enormous trends that would sweep up hundreds of millions of people. The other was to make these trends relevant to business interests. A trend had to be popular, and it had to be profitable. For instance, there was no point in predicting in 1979 that by the year 2000, culture would be more visual than verbal. If you wanted to be a successful futurist, you had to find a way to make a visual culture pay once you made the prediction. You had to turn your trend into a commodity or a service that would make the largest number of people loosen their purse strings. And so the futurists not only began looking for trends that were inherently profit making. They began to define human life in strictly commercial terms. Alvin Toffler has had a genius for that kind of formulation.

Toffler divided history into three "Waves," each Wave characterized in strictly economic terms. In the "First Wave," "most people consumed what they produced." Presumably, Toffler is thinking of early economies, in which people hunted or grew their own food. These people Toffler calls "prosumers," and they lived in an era of "production for use." According to

Toffler, the "Second Wave" was created by the Industrial Revolution. The rise of factories and machines, Toffler believes, separated the function of producer and consumer, dividing humanity into two groups. This was the age of "production for exchange."

Never mind Toffler's shaky grasp of history; never mind, for example, the fact that the most rudimentary economies traded the goods they produced for goods they could not produce—and traded them with people in the same situation. "Production for use"—a solid old Marxist phrase, incidentally—always existed alongside "production for exchange." But Toffler was in the business of selling concepts, not arguing ideas. And his concept of the "Third Wave" was a businessman's dream.

Let's accept Toffler's crude and simplistic definition of what is still the modern economy: an arrangement in which life is divided into producing—that is, earning a living—and buying what other people produce or provide. Though Toffler doesn't say so, in the activity of buying we also find our leisure time. We do so by purchasing a product or a service and then, once the transaction is finished, by withdrawing into our private space to enjoy it. For Toffler, however, a social space in which nothing economic takes place is a terrible waste. It is a kind of sin. He laments:

> All the unpaid work done by women in the home, all the cleaning, scrubbing, child-rearing, the community organizing, was contemptuously dismissed as "non-economic," even though Sector B—the visible economy—could not

have existed without the goods and services produced by Sector A—the invisible economy [that is, the non-remunerative activities of daily life].

Toffler concludes: "Can anyone imagine a functional economy, let alone a highly productive one, without workers who, as children, have been toilet trained, taught to speak, and socialized into the culture?" In other words, the very work of living is wasted time if we do not turn it into an economically productive activity. What most people consider the joy of raising a child—the freedom of raising a child in our own way, after our own instincts—Toffler regards as a failure of definition.

Thus Toffler insists that we become prosumers once again. This is the "Third Wave." We must live as though every niche of existence, no matter how insignificant seeming, can be turned into a commodity or service that someone else will want to acquire. "This casts the whole question of leisure into a new light," writes Toffler. "Once we recognize that much of our so-called leisure time is, in fact, spent producing goods and services for our own use—prosuming—then the old distinction between work and leisure falls apart." Why buy a table and bring it home? Instead, why not buy the parts of a table and bring it home and assemble it? That way, our leisure time gets absorbed into the marketplace—we use our own labor to bring down the cost of the products we consume; in this case, exchanging our personal time and labor for some portion of the price of the table. We produce as we consume; we "prosume."

Even experiences that seem impossible to commodify are candidates for prosumption. Toffler believed that the self-help movement was a Third Wave revolution. Organizations addressing the needs of "smokers, stutterers, suicide-prone people, gamblers, victims of throat disease, parents of twins, overeaters, and other such groupings" allowed people to turn their psychological condition into a unit of exchange. It works like this: I produce my smoking habit for an organization devoted to helping me. They consume my condition in exchange for my money or for funds from another organization. Then they produce their services for me to consume in turn.

The same goes for "experts" who will advise you—in books, lectures, or seminars, on television, CDs, or DVDs—on the most effective way to toilet train your child. In Toffler's bizarre universe, your need to toilet train him becomes a product in the marketplace. The process is the same as with any other type of service that you pay for, with this vital difference: what is being exchanged is an impalpable intimacy, a mental state, or a biological or developmental privacy.

In Toffler's vision of the future, countless activities that were once disinterested and private, or simply leisurely, are converted into one type of transaction or another. Indeed, no private or leisure time exists. Every private thought is performed for public consumption, and every leisure moment (from toilet training to lovemaking) is a highly focused search for a specific gratification, guided by experts serving you in their field. No unexpected events or unanticipated human contact need apply.

It wasn't long before the Internet discovered Toffler. The Web's "users" who are making their own "content" are really Toffler's consumers creating their own products. As with Toffler's smokers and overeaters, the products they are creating are themselves—but in far more numerous and intimate ways than Toffler ever conceived of. Describing the ongoing tale of the YouTuber "Geriatric1927," "a widower, blues fanatic, and former radar technician in the British army" named Peter Oakley, Virginia Heffernan cheered that "YouTube has made room for producers and consumers like Mr. Oakley who have been shut out of earlier pop-culture revolutions." Perhaps people like Mr. Oakley have been "shut out" because the tales they tell are self-indulgently tedious. In any case, Heffernan's effusion perfectly captures the process of prosumerism.

Though Toffler never deliberately set out to theorize about the Internet, it seems the perfect fulfillment of his vision. The Internet certainly loves Toffler—he is quoted throughout books by Kevin Kelly and Fred Turner, to take just two examples. Like Toffler's vision of a world of "prosumers"—a world in which leisure time is saturated with economic urgency—the Internet transvalues all experience into commercial experience.

This is how Adam Cohen, the author of *The Perfect Store: Inside eBay*—and an editorial writer for the *New York Times*—puts it in his valentine to the Internet giant (the "he" is Pierre Omidyar, the founder of eBay):

> By 1995, cyberspace was being taken over by big business, which saw the Internet as little more than a hyper efficient way of selling things. "If you come from a democratic, libertarian point of view, having a corporation just cram more and more products down your throat doesn't seem like a lot of fun," he said. "I wanted to do something different, to give the individual the power to be a producer as well as a consumer."

Omidyar's eBay directly took its cue from Toffler's "pro-sumer"—it has hyperefficiently perfected the art of having people cram its products down their own throats, and all in the transvaluing name of "democracy" and "libertarianism." EBay's producers are its sellers, who are simultaneously consumers of the company's services. But even when you bid for an item in eBay's auction format, you are heating up the competition and raising the price, every bit as much as if you were the "producer" putting the item up for sale. The bidding, however, and the complicated and numerous functions associated with it, feel like play. The online retail giant is the material realization of a Tofflerian world in which leisure becomes seamlessly fused with the busywork of production and consumption.

PACKAGED SELVES

Omidyar's brainstorm was to make shopping a totalizing experience. On eBay, you don't have the same experience as when you go to an actual store. In a store, you pay money for a thing, leave with it, and bound away—you and your purchase—deeper into your private space of leisure time. And when you visit an actual store, shopping is an activity relative to other activities that might run parallel with it: meeting someone new, running into a friend, daydreaming, talking on your cellphone while you browse through the aisles. Shopping online at eBay, however, is not something you can do while your mind wanders. It is an absolute, totalizing experience that fills your mind and appropriates your will.

The solitude of sitting at your computer, and the auction format, and the necessity of keeping your finger at the ready on your mouse, and the countless functions on your screen that seem like diversions but actually serve to keep your attention focused on the act of buying—"related searches"; "buy-now" items; "time left" to bid; "number of bids"; "add to my favorite categories"—all these transform a leisurely activity into an all-consuming one that commandeers the attention as though you were at work. The leisure of shopping becomes an operation that leaves no time for actual leisure. Yet—and this is Omidyar's genius—when you are shopping on eBay, you feel a kind of freedom that you ordinarily experience when at play, even though you have no time to allow your mind to roam away from the business of buying. All the vivid colors, and colorful choices, and the cursor directed by you and your toylike mouse—you might be bankrupting yourself, but you are playing a lively game. "Shopping" on eBay transvalues leisure into work in the same way that people like David Brooks and Stewart Brand have transvalued freedom into commerce.

There is a strange novelty to visiting a site like eBay—once you stop taking the online experience for granted, you realize just how strange it is, especially if you're old enough not to have grown up with it. But there is something even more peculiar about looking to satisfy your desires online in general. No matter how different the Web sites are that you visit, the experience of being on them is similar. Buying a car is different from buying a pair of shoes, and both experiences are different from going to a club to try to hook up with someone. But online just about every experience, no matter how radically divergent one is from the other, is the same. You are sitting (mostly) in the same chair, in the same room, in the same house, using the same computer and the same screen. You are having the most various, and sometimes the most fundamental, experiences in an environment that never changes.

Let's go together, you and I, to eBay. I want to look for a watch. I click on watches, and the screen tells me that currently 106,474 of them are for sale. I scroll down the first Web page, and then another, and another. Ah! What is that? I like the way it looks: slim, elegant, original. I click on the picture. It is a Hublot; next to it appears a descriptive phrase in quotes: "elegant medium." I click again and scroll down the page to search for more details. This item, I am told, has the following qualities: "stainless steel, 18K White Gold/dia. bezel, black rubber deployant strap, silver dial, automatic date, sapphire crystal, water resistant, 50m, 32mm." The watch is in "Pleasant Hill, California, United States." What to do, what to do. I adjust the chair I'm sitting in so that the lumbar support is a little stronger; I also drop the seat down a few inches because my back hurts if I look at the screen at too sharp a downward angle. I take a sip of coffee and consider. Various options are before me. The screen tells me that I have one hour and twenty-nine minutes to make a bid. This means I'd better act fast, obviously; the Hublot is very attractive, and it must be getting dozens, maybe hundreds, of bids. Or I could "email [the Hublot] to a friend" if not interested myself. I could move the Hublot to "add to favorite sellers," too. If I want, I could "get alerts via Text message, IM or Cell phone." I could "view seller's other items" or refine my search. Whatever I decide to do, I should do it quickly. Other people are bidding, and the minutes are ticking away.

Well, I really should relax. I still have over an hour to make a bid. So I switch gears a little and click on Match.com, probably the Internet's most popular dating site. I want to look for a woman. I click on "men looking for women." The screen tells me that currently there are thirty-two pages of women looking for men. I scroll down the first Web page, and then another, and another. Ah! What is that? I like the way she looks: slim, elegant, original. I click on the picture. Her name is Maeve; next to her appears a descriptive phrase in quotes: "Pretty Pisces Seeks . . ." I scroll down the page to search for more details. Maeve, I am told, has the following qualities: "Divorced, White/Caucasian, Slender, Christian/Catholic, Social drinker, maybe one or two, 5′ 7″ (170cms)." She is in "New York, NY, United States." What to do, what to do. I adjust the chair I'm sitting in so that the lumbar support is a little softer; I also raise it slightly because my neck hurts if I look at the screen at too sharp an upward angle. I take a sip of coffee and consider. Various options are before me. The screen tells me that she has been "active within 24 hours." This means I'd better act fast, obviously; she's very attractive, and if she's online so frequently, she must be getting dozens, maybe hundreds, of inquiries. Or I could "Forward her to a friend" if not interested myself. I could "Add her to favorites," too. If I want, I could "send an email, get notified when your match reads it!" I could "See more like her," or refine my search. Whatever I decide to do, I should do it quickly. Other men are interested, and the minutes are ticking away.

"Maeve" has her own unique life. I'm not disparaging her attempt to find companionship in a world where people become ever more cut off from each other, even as life becomes more crowded and accelerated. But on Match.com, she and I are learning to perform ourselves, and package ourselves, and sell ourselves to each other. We sound like everyone else, and like everything else. How did the egalitarian, self-expressing, hierarchy-busting, anti-exclusive Internet end up standardizing its users?

A FEW QUICK WORDS ABOUT
OUR FRIENDS, "CHOICE" AND "ACCESS"

Years ago, when I was in graduate school, I occasionally taught English to new immigrants from the former Soviet Union. Almost all of them told the same story about their first days in America. They went to a supermarket, saw the cornucopia of merchandise, and passed out. Maybe not all of these theatrical storytellers actually lost consciousness, but as refugees from an impoverished, spartan economy, they all shared an unbearable joy at the sight of teeming shelves.

For them, "choice" wasn't simply a marketing pitch. Choice, variety, "options," as we like to say, meant something sacred. Having a single style of clothes or furniture imposed on you, or a single brand of cereal or coffee, is not far removed from an earlier stage of humanity when people clothed and fed themselves with what nature sparsely offered. (That might be one reason why the Soviets loved Jack London's survivalist tales.) Being able to choose what you wear and eat is, in essence, a spiritual advance away from dependency on nature—as well as away from dependency on the state. It is a small but important fulfillment of your uniqueness as a person. In the little dreamspaces called clothing stores, I first realized, as a teenager, that I could live a larger life than the one I was born into.

But it wasn't just choice that thrilled the Russian immigrants. American retail offered another liberating quality. They could buy something they wanted without waiting on line. In the communist Soviet Union, Marx's vision of history's long march toward human freedom degenerated into endless waiting to buy a chicken, or a pair of socks. Since we are mortal beings, time is precious to us. There is something almost caring about a social order that offers "access," that respects the urgency of having time to ourselves.

So you might say that "choice" and "access" are the American space-time continuum. Choice, especially in the realm of fashion or taste, enables us to turn a conception we have of ourselves into a reality in the social space. We dress a certain kind of way, or develop a liking for a certain kind of music, and we move into a different social circle. We make more of the space around us ours, in the same way that "access" to a commodity or service makes more of the time around us ours. Access means time saved in searching to find a thing, or in waiting for it to become available—as well as, of course, the ability to possess something or to participate in something. This is the bright side of a prosperous consumer society. Ironically, it offers us the possibility of living apart from the marketplace's pressures and imperatives by allowing us to carve out our own time and space inside it.

The Internet, however, has twisted "choice" and "access" against themselves. It offers choice purely for its own sake. On the Internet, choice and access lead us to more choice, and more, and more—so that we are buying into the concept of available choice rather than making a specific, concrete choice. The off-line world is also overwhelming in its availability and choices, but the physical boundaries of space-time inexorably intervene. On the Web, space and time barely exist as barriers to satisfaction.

And to actually choose—a Hublot, or a Maeve—and then to stop looking is to limit your experience of the Internet. There must be more Hublots, and more Maeves, more "links," more "alerts," more "forwarding to a friend," more "favorites," ad (so to speak) infinitum. A man's browser should exceed his clicks, or what's an Internet for?

On the other side of the equation, if you are a Hublot or a Maeve—if you are the "seller"—a funny irony takes place. Amid all these infinite-seeming choices, the only way to stand out and be chosen is, paradoxically, to sound more and more like everyone else. But you must sound more like everyone else than anyone else is able to sound like everyone else. You must be the most typical choice in a crowd of choices—the degree of your typicality guarantees your normalcy, and thus the safety of choosing you, in a virtual world where physical presence does not exist as a guide to sanity or safety. At the same time, like the YouTube self-expressers, you are relying on familiar formulas and recognizable styles of self-presentation to gain popularity.

Internet boosters claim that they're the champions of a new age of "demassification." By that, they mean that they're allowing individuals to create their own cultural and commercial choices. But what they've really created is a more potent form of homogenization.

E PLURIBUS UNUM—DARKLY

Not surprisingly, "demassification" is another Toffler-coined term. "Choice" and "access" are its twin war cries.

What Toffler means by demassification is pretty simple. He cites as examples the proliferation of radio stations catering to ever more specialized musical tastes; the rise of neighborhood newspapers (some of them known as "shoppers" in the 1970s); citizens band radio (remember those? they were the first blogs); and, most significant of all, cable television. For Toffler, demassification signifies the end of "standardization" and a new dawn of individuality and "cultural diversity." No longer will we have our cultural choices imposed on us by three television networks, a handful of radio stations and a few movie studios. Every taste we have will be gratified by a new niche that serves it. Not only that, but culture will be the realm where the "prosumer" will thrive most of all. We will create our own marketing niches. Toffler believed that video recorders, for example, would "make it possible for any consumer to become, in addition, a producer of his or her own imagery. Once again, the audience is de-massified."

By now, you've probably become acquainted with the concept of demassification whether you've heard of Toffler or not. Since blogs and Web sites are the perfection of prosumerist fusion, as well as of demassification, the rhetoric promoting the Internet over the past ten years has become saturated with the idea. When the Internet guru Kevin Kelly writes that the Web is "a bunch of dots connected to other dots—a cobweb of arrows pouring into each other . . . [whose] members are highly connected to each other, but not to a central hub," he is describing a Tofflerian network of demassified niches, all of them unified by their submersion in what Kelly calls the marketplace's "Hive Mind."

It's amazing how Internet boosters and their associates, so obsessed with being cutting-edge and with having one foot always in the future, reiterate ideas that are over thirty years old. James Surowiecki's *The Wisdom of Crowds*, in its emphasis on a consumer- rather than a producer-directed society, also updates Toffler's notion of a totally economized life. Chris Anderson's *The Long Tail*, (briefly) the bible of Internet commerce, is the most direct product of Toffler's theories. For Anderson, the marketplace is composed of an infinite regression of specialized niches. Lots and lots of obscure items, taken all together, make even more money than blockbuster single items. In other words, Amazon.com needs its rare and out-of-print titles—as many as it can get—as badly as it needs *The Da Vinci Code*. Everyone has a place at the table.

But what kind of table is it? What happens when you are "producing" your own imagery on your camcorder or digital camera? If it's just for yourself, your family, and your friends, then it's too highfalutin to call yourself a "producer." You're just having fun. However, if you're uploading your "images" onto the Web—on your blog or on a site like MySpace or YouTube—then you're probably hoping to be seen and noticed, and maybe recognized and acclaimed. Expecting that your images will be "consumed" by strangers who will satisfy your self-interest, you are indeed a "producer." Your playful leisure time acquires the rational, calculating, self-conscious quality of labor in the marketplace. Like the members of the WELL, you are customizing your private moments for the edification of potential buyers.

What's more, as niches become increasingly specialized, a greater number of experiences are absorbed into the commercial realm. Alongside the truly marvelous and enriching Web sites catering to just about every human interest—painting, film, butterfly collecting, midwifery, stock investment, model trains, idealist philosophy, and on and on—are those that exploit every kind of emotional, psychological, and sexual intimacy. Demassification has made areas of privacy and intimacy that always stood apart from the marketplace part of it. The saddest personal experience, the most outrageous sex act, the most blatant insult, gets "produced" as a video clip or blog entry for worldwide consumption. Demassification is a more advanced means of allowing mass culture to reach down deeper into life. Product and producer get enfolded into the single individual, who then goes public in order to tout his privacy. He does this in what is becoming the Internet's standardized language of performing, packaged selves. Thanks to the revelation of his most intimate thoughts and memories, Peter Oakley is now working with Mike Hedges, the U2 producer, on Oakley's first album, having just made his first music video. Peter Oakley brought "Peter Oakley" to market the way farmers bring a head of lettuce to market; he sold himself the way songwriters sell their songs. Oakley's very life became his product, rather than something—a song, a table, a new kind of napkin ring—that he made in the course of his life.

NOTHING SUCCEEDS LIKE
(COPYING SOMEONE ELSE'S) SUCCESS

Giant conglomerates now own vast social-networking sites like MySpace and YouTube, and the eyes of other conglomerates—in the realm of television and film, for example—are upon them. Therefore, more and more users on these sites operate with an eye to material advantage. The most startling "candor" is really the most ingenious performance of candor.

No wonder so many "hoaxes" are exposed on YouTube. You begin to suspect that for every hoax that gets uncovered, there are dozens, maybe hundreds more that go undiscovered. You then begin to suspect that the hoaxes that do get uncovered are meant to be uncovered, and that the encouragement of fraudulence and the exposure of fraudulence make up a bur-geoning new form of entertainment. (Its effect on public life is incalculable—accustomed to fading truth in culture, we become inured to it in politics.) A perfect example of "The Genuine Hoax" is the YouTube clip called "Guy Catches Glasses with Face," which portrays one young man throwing a pair of Ray-Ban glasses onto another young guy's face across a room, off a bridge, into a moving car, etc. The clip was, in fact, an ad pro-duced by Ray-Ban itself, but the hundreds of thousands of peo-ple who saw it before the hoax was exposed thought it was real. The discovery of the hoax, however, made the clip even more popular. The ad's fraudulence was the essence of its appeal: see-ing through it thrilled the audience, for whom the transparent fraudulence of media images is perhaps a cathartic antidote to a world dominated by media images. And seeing through a deceit is a tremendous empowerment.

Aware that lucrative vested interests are looking over their shoulders as they "play" online, people end up competing with everybody else, looking over their shoulders at the competition as they "do their own thing." Which is to say—and to repeat—that fewer and fewer people are doing their own thing. They are cautiously and calculatingly imitating someone or something else.

How do you attract worldwide attention on YouTube? How do you become, as the Netties so weirdly call it, a "viral personality"? There are no guidelines in this free-for-all, no precedents to look to. It is different from the old world of so-called mass culture. Then people trying to make a splash in pop culture worked in clearly defined fields like music, or film, or television. The audience for each medium knew its history, traditions, and development. Elvis Presley was aware of Johnny Mercer; the creators of *Friends* knew *The Dick Van Dyke Show*. A songwriter or TV scriptwriter could succeed only by building on his predecessors and then adding his own original twist.

But in the chaos of YouTube and similar sites, you are not competing in a clearly defined field with its own history, traditions, and development. There is nothing against which to measure your "act." That might seem like a liberation. But without the comparative standards offered by antecedents and predecessors, the effect of such chaos and randomness is to induce a general insecurity, and to make conformity the only standard for success. I go to YouTube now and watch a videoblog called "Amazing Child Drummers." How can I judge whether it's "good" or not? It's what they used to call in the days of vaudeville a novelty act. You judge it by its superficial newness, not by its originality. And because novelty is often eye-catching form and no substance, every novelty act resembles the other in some way. "Amazing Child Drummers" might sound different from other YouTube videoblogs like "The Arreola Twins—I Want to Hold Your Hand," and "Cute Boy Singer: Vlad Krutskikh," and "and I love you live by duo guitars—original song by mr. children." But it sure does look like them. They are all united by a quality of self-deprecating sweetness that pleads for attention by accentuating its own ridiculousness.

All the imitation and derivation stem from the fact that on the Internet, success—like choice and access—exists for its own sake. Since the greatest success is, well, being greatly successful, you choose a performance that's already been certified as being a big success. Popularity being the best guarantee of success, you end up imitating the most proven popular act. You must sound more like everyone else than anyone else is able to sound like everyone else. The Ray-Ban ad provoked dozens upon dozens of derivative responses.

How do you know if the act you have chosen is popular? You go straight to the most important part of any YouTube videoblog: "Views." At the moment, "Amazing Child Drummers" has 117,708. The last thing a budding young song-writer wished to do in 1964 was write an imitation of "I Want to Hold Your Hand." In 2008, you put a musical farting cow on YouTube, and within days the Web will bloom with musical farting geese, chickens, and goats. It used to be that performers strove to create excellence and originality within a popular style. They competed against each other's work. Now, if you're a self-expresser looking to find fame and fortune on the Web, you strive only to be popular. You compete against other, measurable degrees of popularity. You strive to come as close to reproducing a successful "original" as possible.

Jonathan Coulton, a computer programmer turned Internet musician and songwriter, told a reporter that when he couldn't come up with a guitar solo for a song he was performing on his blog, he asked readers of his blog to send in their own recordings. Coulton put them up for a vote, and then inserted the winning selection into his song. You might describe that as style by consensus.

THE INTERNET:
MASS CULTURE FOR THE FIRST TIME

In 1957, the sociologists Bernard Rosenberg and David Manning White published a landmark anthology called *Mass Culture: The Popular Arts in America*. Containing essays by figures like Dwight Macdonald, George Orwell, José Ortega y Gasset, T. W. Adorno, and other leading intellectuals, *Mass Culture* was a crystallization of educated opinion on its subject.

The book's impressive contributors were divided into pro and con camps, with the latter being in the majority. In his introductory essay, Rosenberg presented the hostile position, writing that "at its worst, mass culture threatens not merely to cretinize our taste, but to brutalize our senses while paving the way to totalitarianism." Rosenberg lamented what he regarded as mass culture's "sameness" and its "standardized" quality; its two basic assumptions that "everything is understandable" and "everything is remediable"; its "implication of effortlessness.

Shakespeare is dumped on the market along with Mickey Spillane."

White expressed the opposite view. He reminded readers that Germany's exaltation of high culture didn't prevent the barbarism of the Holocaust. He went on to point out that mass culture in his day was rich and diverse, and that it succeeded in bringing serious art and thought to more and more people. Rather than stifling reading or an appreciation of classical music, technology was causing an explosion in the publication of serious books and the production of serious recordings. In 1969, when the two co-editors published a second anthology revisiting the subject, their arguments divided along the same lines.

A half century later, the debate between Rosenberg and White seems as quaint as it is numbingly familiar. They were both right, of course. What they meant by "mass culture" was what you might call a pendular originality that swung between responding to and shaping public taste. It was true that this "mass culture" gave the impression that the most difficult art was "understandable," and the most intractable human problems "remediable." Yet it also brought enjoyment of art and the awareness of intellectual complexity to more people than ever before. Like the Internet, postwar mass culture was both blessing and curse in evolving proportions. But unlike the Internet (so far), it gave rise to a critical scrutiny that hastened the development of its positive aspects. About one thing, however, Rosenberg and White were wrong. Not in 1957, or in 1969, or at any time before the present moment was there such a thing as mass culture.

Through the 1950s, 1960s, and 1970s, there was culture for the masses, yes. It was turned out by the giant record companies, and by the book publishing companies, and by mass circulation magazines like *Life,* and *Look,* and *Time,* and *Newsweek,* and by the comic books (they particularly agitated Rosenberg: "so frightful a juxtaposition of words as 'war comics' and 'horror comics' may be found in our new lexicon"). There were the Big Three television networks, and the handful of Hollywood studios, and, compared with now, a limited number of radio stations, all commercial. But culture for the masses is not the same thing as culture by the masses.

No viewer in 1957 could respond to *The Honeymooners* with a mash-up of the series—a re-editing—in which the viewer himself appears in a scene with Ralph Kramden. No one in 1969 could push a button, click a mouse, and become a "viral personality" recognized around the world. No one until about ten years ago could wake up in the morning, drag himself over to his computer before even getting dressed, and reach more people in his bathrobe with his private thoughts than William Faulkner, at the height of his renown, ever did. No one could go to his encyclopedia and rewrite the entry on William Faulkner (and have that rewritten entry appear simultaneously in every copy of that encyclopedia in the world). For the first time in human history, we are all, as McLuhan, Toffler, and Pierre Omidyar might put it, producers as well as consumers. That is mass culture.

"Mass" is the operative word. Contrary to Toffler, Omidyar, and all of their online acolytes, Web culture is not a gigantic onset of variety, randomness, and individuality. In allowing every individual to appeal to the mass, the Internet is forging, in every "producing" individual, a mass consciousness. (Or as Kevin Kelly hopefully asks, "What is contained in a human that will not emerge until we are all interconnected by wires and politics?") The obsessive use of "wanker" as an insult on the respected political blog Eschaton echoes the references to masturbation on Webnaughty.com. In pornography, "money shot" is that moment when the camera closes in on an ejaculating penis. Andrew Sullivan derived from that strikingly ugly phrase—it is a perfect transvaluation of eros into commerce—the term "money quote," and began using it on his widely read blog when he wanted to refer to the essential point of an article or argument. Hilariously, the entire blogosphere now also uses "money quote" or "money shot" in the same way, though I would bet my hard drive that many of the people who toss these repellent little expressions around have no idea of their origins. Mark Sarvas, for example, on his popular literary blog, The Elegant Variation, awkwardly tells readers that the "money shot for our taste" is that a Ken Follett novel was Germany's third most popular work of literature.

In 1957, when Rosenberg and others worried about popular culture's totalitarianizing effect, you had abstract expressionism, cool jazz, film noir, beats, and hipsters. All these highly individualistic forms of expression grew in the vast spaces in and around culture for the masses, like wildflowers in the shade of a public garden. Their practitioners started out in private, in art or music school, or at a desk alone in a room. They started out in the context of discipline, work, and ambitious yet disinterested curiosity. Their desire to please and to be acknowledged existed alongside their private exertions in their craft.

But in the pre-Internet age, whether you were watching a sitcom or listening to Miles Davis, there came a moment when you turned off the TV or the stereo, or put down the book or magazine, or came home from the theater, or the opera, or the movies. You stopped doing culture and you withdrew—or advanced—into your private social space, or into your solitude. You used the phone. You went for a walk. You went to the corner bar for a drink. You made love with your wife or husband or girlfriend or boyfriend. You wrote a letter.

Now, more often than not, you go to your computer and online. There you log on to a social-networking site, make an entry on your blog, buy something, try to meet a romantic partner, maybe have sex. Or a kind of sex. You might send an e-mail, but no one ever just sends an e-mail. If a Bach fugue went to sleep and dreamed of being another form of communication, it would be the Web. Every online activity leads to another online activity. Then, too, you almost definitely will be on a site that you paid to join, or that is sponsored by a large corporate entity which keeps the site interesting in all sorts of artificial, manipulative ways.

With the Internet, culture—I define culture broadly as any shared public expression—never ends. In 1957, Rosenberg and White both worried about what modern people would do with their growing amount of leisure time. A half century later, hundreds of millions of online performers are putting their leisure time up for sale—the Web site owner or blogger who wants to be heard, the videoblogger desperate to be seen, the Facebook or MySpace person advertising his or her qualities to potential friends, the eBay seller, the Match.com romantic aspirant, and on and on.

For over a hundred years, high culture has been merging with popular culture. But now all *experience* is available as a form of culture. Which means that there are no criteria for judging these disjointed echoes of each other except their popularity. And what drives popularity is a routine's success in merging with the mass, in extending the most generic and derivative appeal. You must sound more like everyone else than anyone else is able to sound like everyone else. Exaggeration, intensification, magnification of proven success, become highly effective means to success. The loudest, most outrageous, or most extreme voices sway the crowd of voices this way; the cutest, most self-effacing, most ridiculous, or most transparently fraudulent voices sway the crowd of voices that way. A friend of mine calls this "mega-democracy," meaning democracy about to tip through perversion of its principles into its opposite. I call it democracy's fatal turn.

PART TWO

4

The Context of Participatory Culture

TO READ THE INTERNET boosters is to get the impression that not only did the Internet spring from nowhere, without influences, but that the Internet itself is the most powerful influence on culture and society today. Yet we don't hear much at all about what cultural circumstances made the Internet possible.

In his book *Playing the Future: What We Can Learn from Digital Kids,* Toffler heir Douglas Rushkoff enthusiastically describes how the Internet has actually created a new type of being: children who are ripe receptors for the latest entertainment technology. Rushkoff declares that the Internet has made teenagers "the latest model of human being equipped with a whole lot of new features." Leave aside the eerie mechanistic idiom, not to mention the outlandishness of Rushkoff's claim. If the Internet really had created a new type of human being, did it do so all by itself, in a social and cultural vacuum?

As it is for so many advance men for the Web, it's certainly in Rushkoff's material interest to portray the Internet as a kind of self-created deity, an unmoved mover. On his personal blog, Rushkoff affects the kind of Internet utopianism Stewart Brand once pretended to and laments the rise of corporate culture: "The topic of my appearance will be the influence of market forces and gentrification on community, segregation, and local values—as well as what is the greater social cost, if any, of participation in real estate market-mania. This will be the first interview related to a book I'm just beginning to write (the proposal is going out this week, in fact) about the rise of 'Corporatism' as America's value system." And on Time.com, he complains that "the Internet became the domain of businessmen." At the same time, he writes books like *Playing the Future* that preach the commercial potential of the Internet, and he receives up to seventy-five hundred dollars an hour from corporations that pay him to instruct them on ways to use the Web to get inside the heads of their youngest consumers. According to the *New York Times*:

> When consulting, Mr. Rushkoff plays the role of impatient youth to the hilt. To meet with the Discovery people, he wore jeans, skateboard-style Simple sneakers and a bowling shirt. He flew to Washington from his New York City home for two 90-minute talks over two days, pocketing around $15,000.

"Sometimes I feel I'm not really saying anything, like I'm a fake," Rushkoff told the *Times* reporter. "Then I realize I'm not paid because I know social science." Which is true. Rushkoff is paid to tell corporate executives who live in terror of an uncertain future exactly what the future requires. But why are they in terror of the future? Because people like Rushkoff tell them that the future consists solely of the Internet, whose true esoteric nature only Rushkoff can explain.

Rushkoff's rival techno-hustler Steven Johnson has an antithetical approach to Rushkoff's, which amounts to the same type of strategy. In *Interface Culture: How New Technology Transforms the Way We Create and Communicate,* Johnson locates, with pretentious adolescent verve, the sources of the Internet in the Victorian novel, medieval urban planning, and silent film, not to mention a philosophical tradition that extends "from the stable, unified truth of Kant and Descartes to the relativism and ambiguity of Nietzsche and Deleuze." For Rushkoff, the meaning of the future lies hidden in Da Vinci–code-like patterns in the present; for Johnson, it lies hidden in Da Vinci–code-like patterns throughout the past. In both cases, the future is an Internet-shaped mystery that only knowledge of the Internet can unlock.

According to both men, the Internet's sources can only be understood in relation to the Internet. Johnson discusses Kant's concepts in terms of Microsoft's "windows." The "whole lot of new features" with which Rushkoff's "latest model of human being" is equipped are all Internet-derived. But like every other technological innovation, from the printing press to television, the Internet took hold in the culture only when the culture was ready to give it a home. If you really want to find the origins of the Internet, you have to look away from it.

Unfortunately, what you'll find is that Web culture, as it exists today, has been shaped by some of the slickest, most utilitarian forces in the larger culture. That's why people like Rushkoff and Johnson insist on talking about the Internet exclusively in terms supplied by the Internet. That's why, in her best-selling history, *Where Wizards Stay Up Late: The Origins of the Internet,* Katie Hafner does not make a single reference to any cultural or social reality outside her subject's narrow parameters—which is like writing a history of television without referring to what has appeared on television. As Jaron Lanier puts it in "Digital Maoism," an essay that decries what Lanier calls "online collectivism":

> The beauty of the Internet is that it connects people. The value is in the other people. If we start to believe that the Internet itself is an entity that has something to say, we're devaluing those people and making ourselves into idiots.

The problem, as we shall see—and as Lanier, himself an energetic booster who belongs to Stewart Brand's Global Business Network, cannot bring himself to acknowledge—is that what the Internet hypes as "connectivity" is, in fact, its exact opposite. But when Lanier criticizes people—like Rushkoff and Johnson—for talking about the Internet as pure technology without a social or cultural meaning beyond the Internet, he's poking a hole in the Internet's orthodox insularity.

POPULARITY FOR POPULARITY'S SAKE

As we've established, popularity is Web culture's Holy Grail. Its supreme importance recalls very familiar experiences.

You remember high school. Everybody wanted to be liked

by everybody else. The very word "like," as preposition and verb, implies a connection between sameness and affection. When you're an adolescent, to be like someone is often a prerequisite for being liked by that person.

There were different ways to conform, to court popularity. You could play up an inherent trait and look for people with similar qualities. Funny people might end up in the drama club; physically strong people might come together in the weight lifters club; fearless craziness could get you in with the mountain climbers or skiers; people with an aptitude for argument or ideas would get drawn together into law or science clubs. Or you could meld yourself to a social clique based on shared interests: jocks, brains, nerds, or geeks. You could even conform to a group of people who specialized in not seeming to care about conforming. Those were the "cool" kids. Yet you didn't just mold yourself to other people's interests, talents, or skills. You used your own interests, talents, and skills to gravitate toward—or attract—people who shared them. And out of the conformist cliques based on some type of talent or skill would come the perfection of that talent or skill. Then came work, and accomplishment, and rewards, all of which reduced the pressure to conform almost to the point where it didn't exist. You conformed along the lines of who you were and what you did best, and after a while your substance as an individual replaced the need to conform. The singularity of your personality and achievements attracted people even more than your reassuring resemblance to them did. You became an adult.

But there was always one type of person who didn't belong to any particular group. He belonged to every group. He—or she—didn't gravitate toward a clique based on a shared interest, or talent, or skill. He gravitated toward any clique that would have him.

Maybe he was the "class clown," who ingratiated himself at the price of his dignity. Or the boy who vandalized or outraged in order to please. Or she was the "easy" girl. Such a person did not appeal to other people on the basis of a quality that he shared with them, a quality that was also the essence of an activity which did not belong to anyone: athletic prowess, dramatic skill, intellectual capacity. Such a person divorced popularity from identity, and from the kind of accomplishment that might boost self-esteem and strengthen identity. He transformed his very self—not his interests, talents, or skills, his *self*—into a product that he tailored to fit the needs of others. For this type of person, there was no such thing as other people to try to relate to. There was only an audience to try to please.

In its fanatical emphasis on the youth market, Internet culture seeks to turn this high-school type into a universal personality. "And, just as in high school, where the cool kids go, the rest of us will follow," confidently writes the *Atlantic Monthly*'s Michael Hirschorn, as he tries to predict the next trend in social-networking Web sites.

In its obsessive stress on youth, however, the Internet plays to the lowest common denominator of youth.

For the person who will do anything to be popular is the most basic kind of person. You could say that he is also the most democratic kind of person, since he depends only on his ability to become like other people rather than on some personal talent that might have the resentment-inspiring effect of making him superior to other people. He is utterly shaped by the majority: What could be more democratic than that?

In this sense, he is a preadult. The Internet loves preadults. When the political blogger Ana Marie Cox—then known as "Wonkette," now the Washington editor of Time.com— wanted to draw attention to herself, she used the word "cunt" to make a point. Which, aside from its titillating quality, is a rhetorical point that anyone could make. What could be more democratic than uttering an obscenity? In a different key, the wish to appeal to the broadest range of people without resorting to complicated thoughts or ideas also drives more serious and responsible political bloggers like Joshua Marshall of TalkingPointsMemo.com: when they want to drive home a particular point, they simply link to other bloggers who have made the same point. Which is an argument everyone has already made. The prerequisite for popularity on the Web is an indiscriminate hunger for popularity, a willingness to use whatever is the most effective means of conformity to gravitate toward— or attract—the largest share of the market (that is, the largest "clique").

LOVE FOR SALE

The term "tipping point" has now become part of our everyday vocabulary. It refers to that moment when an idea, trend, or style "tips" into a craze. Coined by a sociologist in the 1950s and picked up by scientists and marketers since then, the phrase was popularized by *New Yorker* writer Malcolm Gladwell in an essay that he published in the magazine in 1996. In 2000, Gladwell collected that essay and several others in a book called *The Tipping Point,* which immediately became a sensational bestseller.

The book's tremendous success was ironic, since it was *The Tipping Point* that popularized the idea of popularity as the sole criterion of success. Once the "tipping point" became an established concept, the easy hijacking of the Internet by commercial interests was almost a foregone conclusion.

The year 2000 was a significant one for the culture. It was, you will recall, the same year in which David Brooks's *Bobos in Paradise* appeared. In fact, the similarities between the two books are striking.

For Brooks, "detaching oneself from commercial culture means cutting oneself off from the main activity of American life." In *The Tipping Point,* Gladwell takes nearly all of his examples from the ideas of marketing experts, or the behavioral psychologists and economists the marketing companies like to hire. And Gladwell's subtitle, and main emphasis, is "how little things can make a big difference"—"little things" meaning behavioral patterns, social trends, and the like. He puts his faith in laboratory experiments and statistics. Brooks likewise disdains the tendency of postwar intellectuals—the type who appeared in Rosenberg and White's anthology—to have ideas, to deal in "pure reason . . . high-flown abstractions, and towering generalizations." He, too, prefers the little things: "We Bobo types . . . are right to be involved in the world, to climb and strive and experience the dumb superficialities of everyday life, just like everybody else." Just like everybody else. Not, in other words, in an original way.

But the greatest similarity between Brooks's book and

Gladwell's is the exaltation of popularity. For Brooks, the worst thing about America's postwar intellectuals is that the size of their audience is negligible. "The *Partisan Review* crowd was brilliant, but the journal's circulation was minuscule," he writes. It's not hard to share Brooks's lack of enthrallment with the elbows-out, professional squabblers around that legendary postwar journal of ideas. It's impossible to share his reasoning. Compared with, say, the number of people who tune in to Bill O'Reilly or Howard Stern, the readers of Homer, William Butler Yeats, and George Eliot are also "minuscule." To borrow a phrase from Spinoza—not only a nobody by Brooks's standards, but also a shameful generalizer: "All things excellent are both difficult and rare."

The seventeenth-century rationalist philosopher probably wouldn't have cut it with Gladwell, either. For the *New Yorker*'s resident behaviorist, rare apparently means obscure, and obscure means unsuccessful. The only "big difference" that matters to Gladwell is the transformation from obscurity to overwhelming popularity.

Gladwell devotes his book to expounding three ways of winning people over: the "Law of the Few" (you need to find an influential figure to spread your concept); the "Stickiness Factor" (you have to have a catchy concept); and the "Power of Context" (you have to use your environment to manipulate your audience). Gladwell is obsessed with popularity. Back in high school, people like him were the reason you drank, brooded over Kierkegaard's *Fear and Trembling,* and imagined which celebrated public figures would speak at your (imminent) funeral.

On the surface, the phenomenal appeal of Gladwell's book

is one of the biggest puzzles in publishing history. *The Tipping Point* doesn't speak to private concerns. You would think that the average reader would not thrill to tales about how Hush Puppies, *Sesame Street,* Gore-Tex and Glide dental floss, Airwalk sneakers, and the pharmaceutical giant Glaxo Wellcome grabbed the lion's share of their respective markets. Even when Gladwell writes about a social phenomenon like Mayor Rudy Giuliani's successful quality-of-life policing policy in the 1990s, he ends up quoting from evolutionary psychologists employed by business and marketing. Yet *The Tipping Point* has sold millions of copies.

Part of the book's appeal was that presenting a formula for the tipping point captured the American obsession with transformative moments—with "lucky breaks" in romantic, professional, or financial life. But its wild success lay mostly in the fact that Gladwell was writing a guide to making yourself a prosumer. *The Tipping Point* is a how-to book for *Homo interneticus.*

Gladwell has the unsettling habit of describing fads as "epidemics" and of discussing the tipping point in the vocabulary of "infectious disease," "viruses," and "contagion." No one, however, seemed to find it unsettling. The notion that ideas could be compared to viruses was a concept that had already become fairly familiar to the Internet cognoscenti. But coming not long after the AIDS epidemic peaked, Gladwell's book gave the term new widespread currency, converting the terrifying idiom of plague into the happy nomenclature of commercial triumph. It was an adman's dream. In Gladwell's hands, the processes of virus and epidemic were what turned an obscure commodity into a brand name and made it sell, and sell, and sell.

This really was a brilliant transvaluation.

It was, as the Marxists used to say, a "praxis" compared with Brooks's more general transvaluations. For as long as anyone can remember, intellectual culture stood in a skeptical relationship to commercial culture. This is why Brooks takes special aim at the postwar intellectuals, particularly at what he likes to portray as their animus against commerce. But these figures didn't hate commerce, or money. They were very savvy about preserving and advancing themselves. Daniel Bell, one of the most adversarial of the postwar intellectuals, typically had a happy and prosperous career at *Fortune* magazine before moving on to a lucrative position at Harvard.

What cultured, thinking people have been suspicious about since the advent of the written word is the herd thinking that commerce encourages. They fear that the supplanting of independent thought will result in the victory of prejudice and bias, and of the stereotypes that they produce. That it will result in the rule of the mob. Gladwell, however, doesn't fear the mob. Rather, he aspires to bring out the mob-self in the individual. He speaks of "the mistake we make in thinking of character as something unified and all-encompassing." Like that boy or girl we knew in high school who would do anything to please anyone, Gladwell sees other people not as people but as an audience.

He writes, "When we are trying to make an idea or attitude or product tip, we're trying to change our audience in some small yet critical respect: we're trying to infect them." Where the Internet creed is "connectivity," Gladwell's ideal social type is the "Connector." The Connector is a person who knows lots of other people. If you want to win an audience, sell an "idea or attitude or product," you go to a Connector. Because they know a broad range of people, Connectors can be the starting point of a tipping point:

> The Connector belongs to many different worlds—politics, drama, environmentalism, music, law, medicine, and on and on—and one of the key things she does is to play the intermediary between different social worlds.

The sort of person Gladwell describes can certainly be a legitimate and enhancing social figure. He can also be unpleasantly malleable and servile, bending without principle to satisfy the interests of the powerfully placed. Back in the days when even pop sociology—remember William Whyte's *The Organization Man*—challenged mass thinking rather than seeking to promote it, this dark type of "Connector" went by the name "conformist," "operator," "hustler," or "weasel." (That's just to stick to relatively polite terms.) In any event, Gladwell made no distinction.

And no one carped or guffawed when Gladwell actually went on to offer Paul Revere as an early example of a Connector. Being so well connected, you see, Revere knew which doors to knock on during his midnight ride!

In fact, Gladwell's history was as wrong as his ideas were coarse. Revere never made it to Concord, his destination. He was captured by the British and later released. The only reason we remember him is because Longfellow wrote his poem about him, one of Revere's two more successful co-riders having been killed and the other tainted by scandal. You won't find any of those historical facts in Gladwell's falsified version of the midnight ride of Paul Revere.

. . .

In its attempt to bring out the mob-self, to extract and explain the lowest common denominator in every individual, Gladwell's book projects a pinched vision of life. In *The Tipping Point*, human existence is wholly driven by commercial concerns. Life is divided into manipulating winners and manipulatable losers: there are the people who know Connectors, possess a "sticky" concept, and have the capacity to use their environment; and then there is everyone else. (Though one could suppose that Gladwell held out some form of hope: if the manipulated read him carefully enough, they could also learn to manipulate!) Yet Gladwell's charming, almost irresistible anecdotal style made *The Tipping Point* seem like an expression of just the kind of humanistic, belletristic sensibility that the book's own automated values disdained. In a conversation about the design of *The Tipping Point* with—among others—Sarah Crichton, Gladwell's editor at Little, Brown, the *New York Times* reported that in the publishing company's eyes:

> The cover illustration of a single unlighted match suggested highbrow literature or sociology. Presented as a business book, it might have sold even more copies. But Ms. Crichton argued that treating it as a business book would have alienated many readers, while a literary title might sell for many years.

The business book became a literary work by means of the right deceptive image. *The Tipping Point*'s transvaluation succeeded on every level.

Not surprisingly, the Internet boosters love Gladwell. Internet guru Kevin Kelly writes that "there has always been a tipping point in any business, after which success feeds upon itself." In *Who Let the Blogs Out?* Biz Stone, a "senior specialist for blogging at Google Inc.," typically enthuses over Gladwell's ideas: "Connectors are connected. They've got lots of friends." ("Friends" meaning "useful connections.") He excitedly retells Gladwell's (inaccurate) version of Paul Revere's ride and turns Revere into the first blogger, since the latter uses "blogging software instead of a horse to spread [an] idea virus." Stone then goes on to show how Internet users can apply Gladwell's recipes for popularity to their operations on the Web. He gives this example:

> In February 2002 my friend John Hiler used blogging software instead of a horse to spread his idea virus. He wrote a brilliant essay on how bloggers could game Google in such a way that they could push a particular site to the number-one position. The concept is known as "Google bombing" . . . Google displays search results by popularity. When a particular web page has many incoming links, it has a higher PageRank on Google. When all the links to a web page contain the exact same phrase, then Google ranks that page very highly in the search results for that phrase . . .
>
> My friend was the first to write extensively about this trick. At 5:00 A.M., after pulling an all-nighter, he finished his article and emailed it to a colleague for review before posting to their group blog, Corante . . . John woke up to a full-fledged epidemic of his own creation. His article had

generated huge buzz in the blogosphere. Over the next five days more than thirty thousand people read his article; reprint rights to his piece were purchased by *Slate* (a reputable online magazine); and several other publications.

Note the insular nature of Stone's example, which is so characteristic of writing about the Internet: Google's senior specialist for blogging celebrates Internet darling Malcolm Gladwell by telling a story that demonstrates Google's powerful capabilities (under the pretext of showing how Google can be manipulated). Observe also the preadult idiom of "pulling an all-nighter."

But the most striking aspect of Stone's story of Internet success is the example he's chosen to illustrate it. What was it that attracted more than thirty thousand people, that got reprinted in *Slate* and in "several other publications," that "generated huge buzz in the blogosphere"? An article about an original idea, a provocative idea, a masterpiece of style and sensibility and wit, a cry of protest or defiance against some crippling policy or convention? No. The article that generated the huge popularity was an article about . . . popularity. It's like reading Rushkoff and Johnson arguing that the really stupendous thing about the Internet is, well, the Internet.

5

Down with Popular Culture

THE INTERNET'S PREMIUM ON popularity as the sole criterion of success gives the lie to its claims of "choice," "access," and increased opportunity for individual expression. Intentionally or not, Malcolm Gladwell is one of the great facilitators of those deceptive claims. With *The Tipping Point*, Gladwell helped to make the prosumer, the packaged self, and the self publicly performing its privacy not just acceptable social types but desirable ones.

In Gladwell's eyes, the self is always a packaged commodity. It is a product we shape and sell through our performance of what we want other people to think is going on inside us. Like Toffler, Gladwell scorns the idea of leisure time. For Gladwell, we are doing selling work every minute of our waking life:

When two people talk, they don't just fall into physical and aural harmony. They also engage in what is called motor mimicry. If you show people pictures of a smiling face

or a frowning face, they'll smile or frown back . . .
Mimicry . . . is also one of the means by which we infect
each other with our emotions. In other words, if I smile
and you see me and smile in response—even a microsmile
that takes no more than several milliseconds—it's not just
you imitating or empathizing with me. It may also be a
way that I can pass on my happiness to you. Emotion is
contagious . . . We normally think of the expressions on
our face as the reflection of an inner state. I feel happy, so
I smile. I feel sad, so I frown. Emotion goes inside-out.
Emotional contagion, though, suggests that the opposite is
also true. If I can make you smile, I can make you happy.
If I can make you frown, I can make you sad. Emotion, in
this sense, goes outside-in.

If we think about emotion this way—as outside-in,
not inside-out—it is possible to understand how some
people can have an enormous amount of influence over
others.

It's hardly news that the way we communicate with each other
follows evolutionary and behavioral patterns. But if that were
the only influence on the way we communicated with each
other, life would be a lot more simple than it is. In reality, countless other factors influence our encounters and relationships
with other people: temperament, values, belief, ego, sensibility,
mood, the weather, personal chemistry, luck. That's hardly news,
either, to most of us.

Gladwell, however, never gets past talking about rudimentary evolutionary and behavioral patterns, as if we never developed beyond the properties bequeathed to us by our DNA. For

Gladwell, the intended effect elicits the desired response. The most successful people are the most typical: they know how to reproduce the most effective, physiologically tried-and-true facial expressions to get the tried-and-true reaction.

Originality, even if nature made exceptions for it, would therefore be self-defeating. Who wants to take a chance on a gesture or feeling that, because it comes out of nowhere, has a response that can't be quantified and predicted? Anyway, originality is an impossibility. We are overwhelmingly influenced by other people. And by our environment. *You must sound more like everyone else than anyone else is able to sound like everyone else.* The Internet's imperative and Gladwell's credo are identical.

Let's return to the distinction between popular culture and the type of culture fostered by the Internet. Popular culture means just that, culture that has the widest appeal to a broad range of people. That's why popular culture is almost synonymous with ratings: the top-ten hits; the best-seller list; the Nielsens; box-office reports.

But as I suggested in an earlier chapter, originality is an essential part of the creation of popular culture. And originality is, to use Gladwell's uninspiring phrase, "inside-out," something that is generated from within us, rather than being the result of a passive response to something outside us.

Sure, the stimulation of listening to Erroll Garner's percussive left hand stimulated Keith Jarrett's style of playing piano. But Jarrett wasn't just responding to Garner. He was provoked by Garner to discover something deep within himself, something that was wholly his own. Originality is a way of receiving, just as much as a way of creating. Call it "outside-inside-out."

Much has been written about how jazz improvisation is the

exemplary democratic activity. A bunch of guys, working to-gether on the same song, go their separate melodic and rhyth-mic ways while staying in harmony with each other. They draw from what's "inside" them and transform the "outer" form they've been given to work with. Democracy is supposed to be like that, we're told: a nation of individuals bound by the same loose civic ties, each person free to go his or her own way, within the borders of the law. Like the Western sheriff or the urban cop simultaneously at war with the bad guys and with corrupt or indecent superiors, the ideal democratic person in-vents his own conformity. He fits himself into his community, but in his own idiosyncratic way. Think of the Manhattan sky-line and of how each new building, no matter how different it is from the others, immediately becomes part of the evolving con-figuration. The ideal democratic person applies his particularity to his environment in the same way. If he applies it with special intensity, he creates something simultaneously original and har-monious.

Democracy isn't really like that, of course, and we're al-ways caught between, as the poet Paul Valéry once put it, the imperative "to be oneself, yet to be successful." Especially when the greatest success is often the result of following conven-tions more diligently than anyone else. Even the violation of conventions can itself be a rarefied type of convention—insider trading, for example, or a politician accepting campaign contributions in exchange for favors. Inventing your own con-formity is a lot harder in life than it is onstage or on-screen.

But the best of popular culture kept it alive as a condition to aspire to. The history of any popular art is pretty much like the harmonious individuality that you get in a jazz band. It's "inside-out." You rely on a standard form, like the ballad, and you draw from inside yourself to make it your own. "How High the Moon" and "Fly Me to the Moon" might share the same classic song structure of two musically identical verses, a bridge, and then a third verse repeating the first two; they might even share the same lunar imagery—but the two songs don't sound anything like each other. They are as different as the private experiences of their particular composers are different. By the same token, Ella Fitzgerald and Dianne Reeves might both sing "How High the Moon," but their separate versions are as distinct as their personalities. Their separate versions are their personalities.

Or think of Elvis Presley, Jerry Lee Lewis, and Johnny Cash, all working radical changes on the same tradition of country music. Or in film, the almost infinite variations on a type: Brando, Dean, Pacino, Sean Penn, Crowe. Or in television from *The Honeymooners* to *The Mary Tyler Moore Show* to *Friends*, all improvisations on the crude formulas of the sitcom. In every case, the goal is to snatch originality from the jaws of convention by moving from the inside out—from who you are into where you are. The process isn't much different from gravitating toward an established clique in high school along the lines of your individual talent or skill, and then using your individuality to wriggle free from the constraints of the clique.

At least that's the way it has been, until now. There are exceptions, but Internet culture is all about finding a clique or group and striving to reproduce its style with your own adorable, unthreatening, superficial twist. Popular culture used to draw people to what they liked. Internet culture draws people to what everyone else likes. From "I love that thing he does!" to "Look at all those page views!" in just a few years.

UP WITH POPULARITY CULTURE

Pour yourself something to drink, grab a snack, and curl up in your favorite chair. See how *The Tipping Point* became adapted for television as *American Idol*.

Chances are that you've at least heard about this smash hit of a reality-talent show—also referred to as an "interactive reality game show"—which premiered in June 2002 and devotes itself to the goal of discovering "the best singer in the country." Boasting nearly forty million viewers at one point, *American Idol* is one of the most popular shows in American television history.

Here are the details: Tens of thousands of people are screened throughout America; next, thousands more audition in various cities in large auditoriums before the show's three judges: Paula Abdul, Randy Jackson, and Simon Cowell. The few hundred contestants who are left then move on to the second round, in which the crowd is further narrowed down to twenty-four semifinalists. These singers perform on national television, again before the three judges, who choose twelve out of the twenty-four. The final round lasts eleven weeks, and at the end of that time one contestant is declared the winner. Beginning in the second round, viewers are given two hours in which to call in their votes on a toll-free number.

So far it sounds like an updated version of the old-fashioned talent show, not too far from *Major Bowes' Original Amateur*

Hour, a radio program on which Frank Sinatra was discovered in the 1930s—though unlike those humbler days, the winner of *American Idol* gets one million dollars and a deal with a major record label. But there's a radical twist to the performers and their songs on *American Idol.*

Not only does every contestant sing a song already made famous by someone else—every great singer has done that at one time or another. On *American Idol,* nearly every contestant is singing a song already made famous by someone else and singing it in the very same style as that famous person performed it. Or in a pastiche of several famous styles.

You get no sense, watching *Idol,* that fame is built on accomplishment. Success based on achievement has given way to Gladwell's gospel of success based on selling; fame has given way to popularity. As a woman named Amanda Nagurney, who still hopes to one day get herself on *Idol,* put it to *CBS News,* explaining why she admired the people who are chosen to perform on *Idol*: "They just want to be big."

Wikipedia, the collaborative online encyclopedia, trusts its biographical subjects' ranking on the popularity meter more than it does their actions and endeavors. Winston Churchill "was voted the greatest-ever Briton in the 2002 BBC poll of the 100 Greatest Britons." Just in case some readers don't think that steering England through tragedy to triumph in its darkest hours belongs in the Top-Ten Leadership Breakthroughs. Marlon Brando "was named the fourth Greatest Male Star of All Time by the American Film Institute." Franklin Delano Roosevelt "has consistently been ranked as one of the three greatest U.S. presidents in scholarly surveys." These assurances to the reader appear at the beginning of each entry, as if to justify its subject's inclusion in the people's encyclopedia.

Bigness and popularity are all that matter. The reason for popularity is irrelevant. Someone could get big and go "viral" because he has talent, or because he can eat twenty donuts in sixty seconds. When VotefortheWorst.com mischievously seeks to undermine *Idol* by soliciting votes for the show's least talented contestants, it is making a vivid point about the gulf between popularity and merit. Howard Stern's similarly hilarious efforts on behalf of one of *Idol*'s endearingly worst contenders, Sanjaya Malakar, amounted to a kind of social protest against the Gladwellian economicization of culture.

For whereas performers from Bing Crosby to Stevie Wonder—the latter by far the most imitated singer on *Idol*—worked "inside-out," the *Idol* contestants allow themselves to be shaped from the outside in. They allow themselves to be "infected" by proven "viruses." (It depresses me to equate illness with success even in a quotation.) They know that a celebrated style elicits the desired response. They know that there's no guarantee an original performance would get the same response.

It's unlikely that the British creators of *Idol* based the structure of their brainchild on Gladwell's 1996 essay, which introduced the idea of the tipping point to the American public. They didn't need to. The gospel of popularity that Gladwell was identifying, celebrating, and preaching had already taken hold in the culture.

Gladwell's notions make up a large part of what used to be called a "climate of opinion," which the American historian of ideas Arthur Lovejoy once defined as "more or less unconscious mental habits . . . ways of thinking which seem so natural and inevitable that they are not scrutinized." These implicit mental assumptions, Lovejoy believed, make up the "dominant intellectual tendencies of an age." Gladwell simply made these dominant ideas "stickier" than they'd ever been.

What each of *American Idol*'s contestants wants is to create a tide of popularity so strong that it will spur a tipping point of popular opinion that will declare him or her a winner. In fact, the show almost uncannily illustrates Gladwell's three strategies for acquiring universal appeal. The contestants perform before the three judges, who are presented as powerful intermediaries in touch with the most important figures in the recording industry. The winner of each season's competition will be represented by a management company associated with the producers of *Idol*. The judges illustrate Gladwell's "Law of the Few," which decrees that you must find an influential figure—a Connector, for example—to spread the good news about your product.

Like Gladwell's Connector, each judge "belongs to many different worlds": Cowell, the son of a socialite, has had careers in the music industry as producer, consultant, and impresario, and in television; Abdul has made music videos, acted on television and film, and worked as a film producer; Jackson is a musician and record producer. The illusion *American Idol* presents is that if you touch these people, you straddle many spheres of influence; if they touch you, you become "viral." (Yet though *American Idol* performs the principle of the Connector, it doesn't practice it. With the rare exception of the "winner," nobody is going to hook these dancing bears with anybody.)

Then there's Gladwell's "Stickiness Factor." He defines it like this: "Stickiness means that a message makes an impact. You can't get it out of your head. It sticks in your memory." Along with their impersonations of established, market-proven styles, *Idol* contestants add their little quirks in hopes that these eccentric shticks will "stick" in the audience's memory. One performer breaks into nervous laughter; someone else shouts "Can you dig it?" at the judges; another exaggerates his fatal histrionic flaw into a self-consciously outrageous effect.

Yet a quirk is not the same thing as originality. Whether in high or popular art, originality creates a new experience for its audience, whereas a quirk is a novel distraction, not an experience. Elvis's gyrations would have meant nothing without that deep miscegenational voice and that slowly welling emotion verging on parody. After all, nobody who listened to his music at home or in a car saw the gyrations. Elvis's quirky movements onstage were one dispensable element adorning the total experience created by Elvis's gifts. A quirk attracts attention. Originality holds it.

The *American Idol* winners themselves, for all their careful self-presentation, have no style of their own. Walking echo chambers of many pieces of famous styles, they have achieved a kind of spectacular anti-achievement. They are reassuring arguments against the possibility of originality; the most successful among them are the most polished ciphers. Their "stickiness" doesn't lie in their performances. It lies in the offstage revelations of their private lives. This is *Idol*'s triumphant exploitation of the "Power of Context." Gladwell describes his third law as the necessity of being "sensitive to the conditions and circumstances of the times and places in which [epidemics] occur." *Idol*'s creators have a genius for being sensitive to their memoir-soaked environment.

Since it is not just a talent show but a reality program, *Idol* reports on the offscreen lives of its contestants, particularly as they move into the semifinals and then into the final weeks. The transparent blandness of the performances doesn't provide the stickiness. Their function is to keep alive the "democratic" hopes of the audience. Nothing difficult or rare or superior is going on here, these derivative performances seem to say. What is happening is that an ordinary life, demonstrated by its gossipy particularities, has stumbled onto a platform of contagion. It's the gossipy particularities that supply the stickiness. Kelly Clarkson's struggle to live a dignified life is what made her performance of Aretha Franklin's "Respect" so memorable, not her performance of the song. On *Idol*, it's the mediocre singing that provides the occasion for the performance of the life.

Like Toffler's prosumers—like everyone in the world of reality television—*Idol* contestants turn their leisure time into work. Like the people on YouTube and on the social-networking sites, on the Internet dating sites, and in the blogosphere, *Idol*'s striving singers package and perform their privacy for public consumption. What makes this show, this enemy of originality, so original is that the private and the public are literally fused and exposed before your very eyes. In the race for popularity—that is, fame without accomplishment—the self is left behind. They just want to be liked. They just want to be big.

HOW MUCH IS THAT ACTOR
IN THE WINDOW?

On *American Idol,* the audience doesn't merely live through the private contestants' experience of becoming public singers. It decides their fate with a phone call. Watching *Idol,* you can virtually reach out and grasp someone's inner life and pluck it, like a guitar. You never have to surrender yourself to an experience that you can't seize and make your own. We are no longer passive recipients of entertainment. We have become active consumers of it.

Needless to say, this transformation has happened over time. About fifteen years ago, I stumbled across a cartoon that showed a bunch of people on a bus reading the newspaper. Everybody was wearing a baseball cap with his or her name on it: "Bob," "Howard," "Mary." If you looked closely, you could make out the names of the papers they were reading, but none of the names were familiar. In the space at the top of the page, where the words "New York Times," or "Washington Post," or "Wall Street Journal" should have been, you saw "The Daily Bob," "The Howard Times," "Mary's Journal." Things had reached the point, in this cartoon's comical world, where people could not absorb any opinion, thought, or fact that wasn't, literally, about them. (The conceit was not so far from Internet booster Nicholas Negroponte's much later concept of "The Daily Me," in which Internet users customize their news sources so that they only read news that suits their interests and tastes. Bill Gates cheerfully calls this "customized information.")

The cartoon was fancifully accurate. The whole trend in popular art over the past fifteen years or so has been to tell a story that narrows the gap between the spectator and entertainment. Countless television programs now fabricate a fig leaf of passively enjoyed entertainments, and hide behind that a dynamic invitation to get involved in the show as an active, acquisitive consumer. Reality television, with its direct appeal to the viewer's experience, and the viewer's judgment, and sometimes the viewer's vote, is the most obvious such tactic.

More subtly, there are the shows about neurotic detectives, depressed gangsters, conflicted teenagers, dysfunctional couples—that is, shows about us. Earlier television realism created series like *All in the Family, Roseanne, Hill Street Blues, St. Elsewhere,* shows whose "realism" consisted of larger-than-life characters facing more or less ordinary dilemmas of oversized proportions. The dilemmas, no matter how personal, always had a social dimension. Today's television characters are often defined by their troubled mental states. For it's easier for viewers to move into a character's generic psychological problems than to inhabit a character's inevitably alien social and physical environments.

Whatever their virtues, these programs push the boundaries of the familiar. That's why so many of them put their characters on an analyst's couch. Such shows want to ring true deep inside your head. They want to create the illusion that you are right there, inside the characters' heads, all of you, you and the characters, moving through the same familiar problems and dilemmas. We're no longer living through the characters' exciting and exotic adventures. They're living through our boring and mundane daily lives.

When on that old cop show, *Columbo,* Peter Falk's owlish detective wedded a sly, Socratic manner to dogged sleuthing, the originality of his conceit drew us out of ourselves into the eccentric character on the screen. It was hard to identify with Columbo, hard to assimilate his irony, tone of voice, unassuming slouch, and wry smile. The eccentric relationship between him and his quarry, a relationship that brought out Columbo's special qualities, was another distancing element. In the end, you could relish the familiar feelings the show provoked in you, but you couldn't, even for a second, get your mind around Columbo the character and melt into him. He remained a different person from you, solidly strange and impermeable. You sat back and enjoyed the creation of an original experience.

The neurotic detective Tony Shalhoub plays on the crime series *Monk,* on the other hand, exists in a social vacuum. Monk's condition is, as the health insurance companies say, preexisting. It thrives independent of his social environment. And since Monk's condition is medical and not characterological—that is, it could happen to any of us—we can slip right into Monk's character, or he can slip into us. When Monk's obsessive-compulsive detective visits his therapist and describes his familiar-sounding fears and anxieties, he is moving out of the television into our everyday experience. Both *Columbo* and *Monk* are brilliantly done, and thoroughly enjoyable. But they have two very different effects on the viewer. They move in two very different directions.

Just about every television show now has a Web site that invites the viewer-consumer to play an active role in the show. You answer questions about plot or characters, read the characters' blogs, and, of course, vote on something or other having to do with the show. Voting is big on television. It empowers the audience by giving them the illusion of control over entertainments that once were passively enjoyed. On the Web site for ABC's popular medical drama, *Grey's Anatomy*, you can take a quiz that asks: "Which Character Are You Most Like?" It's a form of voting. (You'll also have to read an ad for a vaccine against genital warts. Ask your doctor if it's right for you.)

The effect of such new forms of "access" is a strange one. They abolish the space between you and the screen and literalize the fiction you are watching. You become the center of the entertainment that, traditionally, helped viewers get out of themselves. Entertainment used to be "escapist." Now it's as though everyone who's ever escaped has been pursued, rounded up, and returned to his or her own ego.

The figures you see on the screen are no longer actors playing imagined roles. They are objects to be voted on and absorbed into our own experience. In that way, we acquire and possess them like any other purchasable product—"Which Character Are You Most Like?" The situation in entertainment is not much different from the cellphone technology that lets you point your phone at some material object you desire, so that you may get all the pertinent information about it before you make the decision to buy. Before our various screens, we point our remote, or aim our mouse. Then we grab and we get.

6

Participatory Culture

OF COURSE, CULTURE HIGH and low has always sought to portray experiences that would incite feelings the spectator could identify with. You could draw a line right up to *The Sopranos* from Aristotle's famous dictum that drama must cathartically arouse a universal "pity and terror." Modernism's difficulty and postmodernism's impersonality might have dispensed with catharsis. That, however, had the effect of making vicariousness even more urgent and inventive in popular culture, the best of which has grown more complex as high art has gotten more fractured.

But we have gone way beyond vicariousness.

Walter Pater, the Victorian English critic, once said that all art aspires to the condition of music. Now all popular culture aspires to full viewer participation—not just the TV Web sites, but karaoke, movieoke (in which you substitute yourself for an actor playing a role in an actual film), and the expansion of video-game techniques into what used to be the realm of passive entertainment. Just as the stomach-heaving car chase in *Bullitt* helped inspire the first generation of video-game designers, their inventions wholly shaped car chases like the one in *I, Robot,* in which the spectator is virtually soaring into and through the screen. And for some years now, film stars have been lending their talents to sophisticated video games that allow players virtually to become a character in a movie. At the same time, more and more video games become feature films.

The tendency that American actors have always had to play both a role and their offscreen persona at the same time is a result of the Method theory of acting's insistence on an actor building character out of pieces of his own life. That tendency has now reached a further stage.

These days, thanks to movieoke and video games, a spectator now has various opportunities to play his favorite actor performing his favorite role. The director James Cameron is even reportedly working on a new 3-D film called *Avatar*—also a term for an anonymous Internet user's alias—which will offer to spectators the experience of actually being in the film. Lee Strasberg and Stella Adler, the two principal American gurus of the Method, would have stared in disbelief if you had been able to describe to them this latest phase of American cinematic realism.

Yet the Method is, in fact, one of the chief catalysts that has brought us from popular to participatory culture, just as the movies are the perfect illustration of that radical change.

Start with movies from the 1930s, before the Method began to influence Hollywood after the Second World War. If you watch a few examples from every decade after that up to our own, you'll notice the significant fact that early movies had a stable camera that remained fixed on the social situation.

The camera encompassed every person in the scene, and it showed the characters interacting with each other in a definite, recognizable social setting. That's why close-ups in the 1930s and 1940s and into the early 1950s were so glamorous. They were the exception. The face filling the screen, often suffused with a romantic, soft-focus aura, lifted spectators out of the social realm into the kingdom of dreams. Audiences didn't identify with the large, mythic face. They either vicariously hungered for it or understood that it was an object of other people's vicarious hunger. That cinematic moment, in which the social situation suddenly dissolved into the apparition of a face, had a deep resonance. It exposed the separateness between public and private realms. It said that the dream of ultimate fulfillment which we harbor, deep inside us, was unattainable and remote.

But alone with that hovering dream in the darkened theater, audiences nevertheless felt enchanted, gratified, and consoled. They knew that the other people sitting in darkness around them were having the same experience. Other people were being thrilled by a vicarious hunger, and then experiencing it as an unattainable ideal. For every spectator in that theater, the social setting—kept steadily in view by the camera—was intractably real. It was a shared condition. The dramatic evanescence of that sudden, gigantic face proved it.

With the rise of the Method in American film during the 1950s, all that changed. Strasberg and Adler believed that the effective actor drew from personal memories to provoke in himself a strong emotion, and since emotion is most vividly conveyed by the face, they apotheosized the face. The lifting of an eyebrow, the downward motion of a mouth, could change a plot.

By now, five decades later, the camera no longer stays trained on all the people in a scene, interacting with each other in a definite, recognizable, fleshed-out social setting. The camera moves quickly, or nervously, or distractedly—as if brokering our own easy distraction—from one screen-flooding close-up to another. But unlike the fuzzy, glamorous close-ups of yore, these close-ups are shorn of romance and glamour.

Today's giant cinematic face is functional, real, gritty, pragmatic. The face, rather than the social setting, is the intractable social fact. Now the social setting has become as dreamlike as those old, romantic faces. Quick, can you clearly remember a single physical setting, interior or exterior, in *Mystic River*—except, of course, for the action moment in the park where the body of Sean Penn's daughter is found? You probably can't. But do you have a clear mental picture of the faces of the actors who starred in the film? Sean Penn's functional, real, gritty, pragmatic face, perhaps? I bet you do. Now, you remember the faces of Humphrey Bogart and Ingrid Bergman in *Casablanca*, of course, glamorous close-ups and all. But do you remember the physical settings—the smoke-filled nightclub, Rick's shadowy apartment, the small airfield wrapped in fog. How could you ever forget them?

Nowadays, we don't sit in the darkened theater sharing a vicarious illusion with other people. More likely, we sit in our darkened living rooms or bedrooms before a screen that is filled, not with an unattainable ideal, but with an ordinary face, communicating ordinary, or plausible, emotions. This isn't an apparition from on high. It's another person within our reach. And from this accessible face that seems to be directly relating to us—from this easily habitable face that could just as well be us—it's just one short step to the face we can make disappear with a vote on *Idol*, or digitally interact with in a video game.

With the disappearance from film of a social setting, the social space has become the virtual one occupied by the viewer and the face on the screen. Can you imagine *Casablanca* without Rick's casino, *Father of the Bride* without a staircase, *North by Northwest* without a train's dining car or a sinister mansion's menacing living room? But it is easy to imagine, say, the director Tony Scott's *Man on Fire* without a single one of its settings, save perhaps for—as in *Mystic River*—the action moment, the street where a little girl is abducted and a shoot-out occurs. The movie takes place between us and Denzel Washington's remarkably evocative face. Its only memorable setting is one where action happens—a space that is wholly available to the vicarious insertion of ourselves. This isn't to say that there aren't exceptions. Alejandro González Iñárritu's searing *Babel*, for example, seemed like a deliberate, defiant exercise in embedding the giant cinematic face in vivid physical settings. But such movies are rare—at least for now.

Putting famous actors and celebrities within our reach has created a curious backlash. It encourages us to reject them as famous actors and celebrities, even as the culture becomes increasingly obsessed with celebrities. The ubiquity of the magnified face makes us want to rebel against such an inflation of another person's presence. These outlandish looming presences become onerous. The rise of reality TV, which celebrates physical and psychological imperfection, is a revolt against the oppressiveness of other people's fame—a rebellion against the oppressive authority of those glamorous, unattainable "screen icons."

An even more explicit uprising against glamorous authority is the celebration of mediocre, merely derivative talent on the anti-original *Idol*. Fame is now a "virus" that "infects" the masses by means of its "contagiousness." Popularity has bullied fame out of its perch. The only "screen icons" now are the "avatars," the little screen images that Internet users create to symbolize their online personas. Fame, in its new incarnation as popularity, is supposedly now within everyone's grasp. As the announcer says on *American Idol* about the show's invitational premise: "You ask an entire country to step forward and audition."

Such resentment against the authority of glamour lies behind blogs like AwfulPlasticSurgery.com, where you can find derisive before and after photographs of celebrities thought to have had their features surgically adjusted. On ModiFace.com, you can submerge the features of famous actors in your own face. For a while, if you subscribed to AOL, you could play a little game that allowed you to choose celebrities and then perform plastic surgery on them. You could cut off an erstwhile screen idol's nose, and spite his face, all at the same time.

No one would argue that, on one level, this smashing of idols is a healthy iconoclasm. People simply are choking on unreal images of perfection; they are rebelling against the way consumer society tries to shame them into spending small fortunes to improve their appearance. Being mad as hell and not going to take it anymore is a good old American tradition.

But driving the rebellion against authoritative images is a hatred of any kind of cultural authority, whether it is a hollow, pumped-up star or a talented actor who has worked hard at his craft. And driving the gospel of popularity is an appeal to each one of us to replace the inflated icons with an inflated sense of ourselves—whether we have talent and discipline or not. Web culture's hatred of the famous figure often comes down to an indiscriminate mania for access to what other people have and we don't. It's not the gaseous star we dislike; it's the fact that he possesses a status and authority that we feel we deserve. In this sense, the cult of popularity, which celebrates "you," is instilling in everyone an impulsive impatience with anyone and anything that is not you.

Before long, we won't need to try to share, usurp, or destroy the actors' pretense. Before long, we'll be acting right beside them. The most influential photographer now working is Jeff Wall, who recently had a retrospective at the Museum of Modern Art in New York. Wall's fame rests on huge, life-sized photographs done in Cibachrome, a vividly colored film that resembles cinematographic film. The current generation of photographers has, to a great extent, been shaped by Wall.

Wall characteristically photographs staged scenes that resemble movie stills. You look at them and feel as if you had stumbled upon a moment in a film. But since you aren't seeing this scene in a film, you don't know the story around it. You have to provide it yourself. In her catalog for the show Acting

Out, a 2005 exhibition at the Neuberger Museum of Art in Purchase, New York, that included Wall and his disciples, Kathleen A. Edwards writes that such photographs

> contain all the elements for feature-length, no-holds-barred movies to unfold in the imagination of the viewer ... The photograph's illusory involvement with the photographer/spectator allows the viewer to project him- or herself into the scene in any chosen role ... [Such] photographs make the activity of imagining a scenario just as, if not more, interesting than [*sic*] actually participating in one ... Artists, model, and spectator are collaborators ... and each participant's experience occurs in private contexts under emotional terms.

Restless, impatient, acquisitive, we don't have the time or the mental space to passively allow an aesthetic experience to sweep us into its newness, or its strangeness. We want to jump right in and help do the work of creation. We want *access*. It was always certain musical occasions that made that type of participation possible, from ancient Dionysian rituals to the masque plays of Elizabethan times to, in our own era—if you will pardon an even greater leap—swing to Woodstock to rap. Now it's the more reflective arts, too. If he were starting out today, the photographer Robert Frank, for example, would not be traveling across America, snapping pictures of ordinary life. He would be orchestrating his photographs to look like stories about American life, artificially real stories that we had to mentally project ourselves into in order to complete. And like those cartoon readers of newspapers all about themselves, we can work more efficiently, and possess greater control over what entertains us, if it reflects our familiar experience—if the entertainment "allows the viewer to project him- or herself into the scene in any chosen role." No wonder so many memoirs and novels written in the first person are published: you can slip more easily into an "I" than into the third person. No wonder rhythm has overtaken melody in popular music: it's easier to assimilate rhythm's sameness to your fantasies than to step out of yourself and follow melody's different changes. Rhythm is music's first person, as the close-up is film's.

There was always one chief difference between popular or high culture and commercial culture. The former, even at their crassest and most profit-driven were meant to be enjoyed disinterestedly. Whether you were watching a play by Sophocles, or attending a concert by the Beastie Boys, or reading a book by Danielle Steel, you had no material interest in what held your interest. You were in the experience for the pleasure that comes either from high art's absorption of your attention or from popular art's gifts of diversion. In both cases, you were briefly sprung from the daily pressures of self-interest. You laid yourself and your ego aside, in one degree or another.

Commercial culture, on the other hand, is all about the gratification of your self-interest, and it involves the total engagement of your ego. The success of a commercial transaction lies in your ability to "project [yourself] into the scene" of the transaction. Assertiveness, initiative, full participation in every aspect of the deal that has a bearing on your self-interest—those qualities are what carry the day for a buyer or seller, not passive enjoyment of the situation unfolding before you. At the heart of a successful work of art, high or low, lies something wholly fresh and other, some type of original experience. At the heart of a successful transaction is the satisfaction of your self-interest—at the heart of a successful transaction is you.

With the rise of participatory culture, pop culture has entirely merged into commercial culture. Enchantment of the imagination has given way to gratification of the ego; vicarious transport out of yourself has given way to . . . yourself. It's not just YouTube that's about "you" in this new order of things. It is every cultural experience that is about "you." Welcome to the Youniverse. Welcome to the world of the Internet.

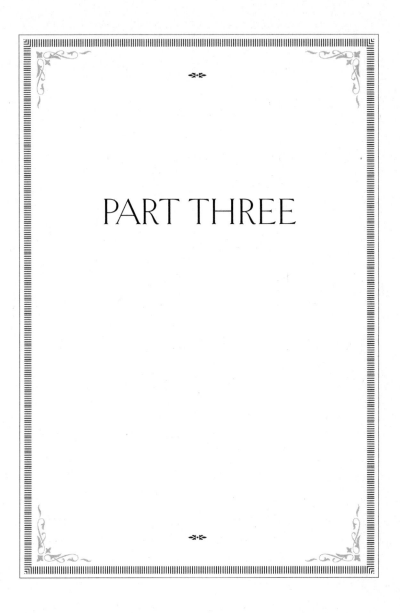

PART THREE

7

A Dream Come True

"WEB 2.0" IS THE Internet's characteristically mechanistic term for the participatory culture that it has now consummated and established as a social reality. In this topsy-turvy galaxy, no person, fact, or event is beyond your grasp.

Web 2.0 is what the Internet calls its philosophy of interactivity. It applies to any online experience that allows the user to help create, edit, or revise the content of a Web site, interact with other users, share pictures, music, and so on. Amazon.com is a product of 2.0 technology because it allows visitors to write their own reviews of books that Amazon offers for sale, and to sell their own used books as well. EBay is 2.0-based because buyers and sellers interact with each other. Web 2.0 rules the social-networking sites like MySpace, Facebook, and Friendster, and also the blogosphere, whose essence is the online exchange of opinions, ideas—and spleen.

Although Web 2.0 is the brainchild of businessmen, many of its promoters extol it with the rhetoric of "democracy," that most sacred of American words. But democracy is also the most common and effective American political and social pretext. While the liberal blogosphere thundered with cries of hypocrisy about Bush's claim that he was bringing democracy to Iraq, no one bothered to peek behind the Internet's use of the word "democracy" to see if that was indeed what the Internet was bringing to America.

Here is Lawrence Lessig, the foremost advocate of Internet freedom in the realm of copyright law, on the Internet's capacity for "capturing and sharing" content—in other words, for offering full participation in the culture:

> You could send an email telling someone about a joke you saw on *Comedy Central,* or you could send the clip. You could write an essay about the inconsistencies in the arguments of the politician you most love to hate, or you could make a short film that puts statement against statement. You could write a poem that expresses your love, or you could weave together a string—a mash-up—of songs from your favorite artists in a collage and make it available on the Net . . . This "capturing and sharing" promises a world of extraordinarily diverse creativity that can be easily and broadly shared. And as that creativity is applied to democracy, it will enable a broad range of citizens to use technology to express and criticize and contribute to the culture all around.

Before you try to figure out what Lessig is saying, you have to get through the Internetese, this new, strangely robotic, automatic-pilot style of writing: "A poem that expresses your love" . . . for what? How do you "express . . . the culture all around"? As usual, the Internet's supreme self-confidence results in lazy tautology: "This 'capturing and sharing' . . . can be easily and broadly shared." And never mind that elsewhere, in the same book—*Free Culture: How Big Media Uses Technology and the Law to Lock Down Culture and Control Creativity*—Lessig defines democracy, strangely, as "control through reasoned discourse," which would seem to disqualify *Comedy Central* from being considered one of the pillars of American democracy.

More telling is Lessig's idea of "democracy," a word that in the American context means government by the people through freely elected representatives. Lessig seems to think it means "creativity," or, as they like to say on the Internet, "self-expression." But even tyrants allow their subjects to write love poems or exchange favorite recordings. The Roman emperor Augustus cherished Ovid for the latter's love poetry—until Ovid's romantic dallying came too close to the emperor's own interests. And only tyrants forbid their subjects to make political criticisms—loving to hate a politician in public is hardly an expansion of democracy. It's the result of democracy. Lessig has confused what makes democracy possible—certain political, not cultural, mechanisms—with what democracy makes possible: free "expression."

Lessig isn't the only one singing 2.0's praises who seems confused about fundamental terms. Jay Rosen, a professor of journalism at New York University, is maybe the most voluble booster of the "citizen journalism" that he believes fulfills the blogosphere's social promise.

Rosen has started a blog-based initiative called Assignment Zero, in which anyone, journalist or not, can file an "investigative" news article. Rosen called this "crowdsourcing" in an interview with the *New York Times*'s David Carr, who reported the story without expressing the slightest skepticism and without presenting an opposing view to Rosen's. And there is an opposing point of view. In the world of Assignment Zero, if you are someone working for a politician with an ax to grind, you could use Assignment Zero to expose a pesky journalist. Or you could just go on the blog to take down someone who has rubbed you the wrong way. No institutional layers of scrutiny, such as exist at newspapers, would be there to obstruct you.

Yet Rosen celebrates the 2.0-based blogosphere for what he portrays as its anticommercial gifts to democracy:

> We're closer to a vision of "producer democracy" than we are to any of the consumerist views that long ago took hold in the mass media, including much of the journalism presented on that platform. We won't know what a producer public looks like from looking at the patterns of the media age, in which broadcasting and its one-to-many economy prevailed.

But we do know what a "producer public" will look like. Alvin Toffler described it thirty years ago. It will look like a totalized "consumerist" society, where everyone's spare moment is on the market and where journalists in the blogosphere will have their every word quantified and evaluated by vigilant advertisers. Where "producers" are simply consumers made more dependent on the marketplace by the illusion of greater participation in the marketplace. On the blog Assignment Zero, the public pays for the stories it wants to see reported. Rosen hasn't escaped the constrictions of commerce. He's made them tighter.

Lessig and Rosen are true believers in the Internet, people who have staked their professional (and economic) futures on its untrammeled success. It's in their interest to confuse American democracy's meaning with what American democracy means to them. *Time* magazine, on the other hand, has no stake in the triumph of the Internet.

Yet like every other "old" media news organization, *Time* is so frightened by the Internet boosters' claims of "old" media's impending irrelevance that for its "Person of the Year" in 2006, it put a picture of a computer screen on the magazine's cover with the single word "You." Then it went on to celebrate Web 2.0 as "the new digital democracy":

> It's a story about community and collaboration on a scale never seen before. It's about the cosmic compendium of knowledge Wikipedia and the million-channel people's network YouTube and the online metropolis MySpace. It's about the many wresting power from the few and helping one another for nothing and how that will not only change the world, but also change the way the world changes . . . Silicon Valley consultants call it Web 2.0, as if it were a new version of some old software. But it's really a revolution . . . We're looking at an explosion of productivity and innovation, and it's just getting started, as millions of minds that would otherwise have drowned in obscurity get backhauled into the global intellectual economy.

Who are these people? Seriously, who actually sits down after a long day at work and says, I'm not going to watch *Lost* tonight. I'm going to turn on my computer and make a movie starring my pet iguana? I'm going to mash up 50 Cent's vocals with Queen's instrumentals? I'm going to blog about my state of mind or the state of the nation or the steak-frites at the new bistro down the street? Who has that time and that energy and that passion?

The answer is, you do. And for seizing the reins of the global media, for founding and framing the new digital democracy, for working for nothing and beating the pros at their own game, TIME's Person of the Year for 2006 is you.

Yes, seriously, who has the time, energy, and passion to make a movie about his pet iguana and broadcast it over the Internet? Who has reached that level of commitment to democracy? Who has the time, energy, and passion to mash up 50 Cent's vocals with Queen's instrumentals, to blog about his state of mind or the state of the nation or steak-frites? *Time*'s encomium to a brave new world reads like a forced confession's rote absurdity.

About one thing, however, *Time* was right. All this so-called play was not play at all. Everyone was getting "back-hauled"—whatever that means—into the "global intellectual economy," though by "intellectual" *Time* meant nonmaterial, mental. Deliberately or not, *Time* was adding its voice to the general gulling of Internet boosterism and giving a helpful push to the facile shift of culture to commerce.

Tim O'Reilly is more explicit about this commercial democracy, if not all that comprehensible. O'Reilly is the head of an Internet company called O'Reilly Media, and he is generally considered the originator of 2.0. To begin with, O'Reilly has a somewhat different view of the blogosphere from Rosen:

> The blogosphere is the equivalent of constant mental chatter in the forebrain, the voice we hear in all of our heads. It may not reflect the deep structure of the brain, which is often unconscious, but is instead the equivalent of conscious thought. And as a reflection of conscious thought and attention, the blogosphere has begun to have a powerful effect.

"It may not reflect the deep structure of the brain, which is often unconscious, but is instead the equivalent of conscious thought." If your toaster could write a sentence, it would write one just like that. O'Reilly goes on:

> First, because search engines use link structure to help predict useful pages, bloggers, as the most prolific and timely linkers, have a disproportionate role in shaping search engine results. Second, because the blogging community is so highly self-referential, bloggers paying attention to other bloggers magnifies their visibility and power . . . like Wikipedia, blogging harnesses collective intelligence as a kind of filter . . . much as PageRank produces better results than analysis of any individual document, the collective attention of the blogosphere selects for value.

PageRank is Google's algorithm—its mathematical formula—for ranking search results. This is another contribution, according to its touters, to access to information, and therefore yet another boon to "democracy." PageRank keeps track of Web sites that are the most linked to—that are the most popular. It is, in fact, the gold standard of popularity in Web culture. What O'Reilly is saying, in plain English, is that the more people blog, and the more blogs link to each other, the more highly ranked the most popular blogs will be. When O'Reilly writes in his appliance-like manner that "the collective attention of the blogosphere selects for value," he simply means that where the most bloggers go, people who are interested in general trends— businessmen and marketing experts, for instance—will follow. "Value" in O'Reilly's sense is synonymous with popularity.

In this strange, new upside-down world, words like "democracy" and "freedom" have lost their meaning. They serve only to repel criticism of what they have come to mean, even when that criticism is made in the name of democracy and freedom.

THROUGH THE LOOKING GLASS

What would you have said if I had told you, ten years ago, that there would soon come a time when anyone with something to say, no matter how vulgar, abusive, or even slanderous, would be able to transmit it in print to millions of people? Anonymously. And with impunity.

How would you have reacted if I had said that more drastic social and cultural changes were afoot? To wit: Powerful and seasoned newspaper editors cowering at the feet of two obscure and unaccomplished twentysomethings, terrified that this unassuming pair might call them "douchebags" in a new gossip sheet called Gawker. An obscure paralegal in Sacramento, California, who often makes glaring grammatical mistakes on his blog, becoming one of the most feared people in American literary life, on account of his ability to deride and insult literary figures. High-school kids called "administrators" editing entries in a public encyclopedia, entries that anyone, using an alias, could change to read in any way he or she wanted. Writers distributing their thoughts to great numbers of people without bothering to care about the truth or accuracy of what they were writing; writers who could go back and change what they wrote if they were challenged—or even delete it, so that no record of their having written it would exist.

You would have laughed at me, I'm sure. Maybe you would have thought that I was purposefully and ludicrously evoking Stalin, who rewrote history, made anonymous accusations, hired and elevated hacks and phonies, ruined reputations at will, and airbrushed suddenly unwanted associates out of documents and photographs. You might have said, What point are you trying to make by saying that our American democracy is moving toward a type of Stalinism? How trite, to compare American democracy to its longtime nemesis using crude inversions. Are you some sort of throwback to the anti-American New Left?

And what if I had, to your great irritation, persisted and told you that anyone who tried to criticize one or another aspect of this situation would immediately be accused of being antidemocratic, elitist, threatened by change, and pathetically behind the times? If I had told you that in fact, because of these risks, few people ever did offer any criticism? The gospel of popularity had reached such an extent in this upside-down world that everyone, even powerful, distinguished people, cringed at the prospect of being publicly disliked.

What I've been describing is the surreal world of Web 2.0, where the rhetoric of democracy, freedom, and access is often a fig leaf for antidemocratic and coercive rhetoric; where commercial ambitions dress up in the sheep's clothing of humanistic values; and where, ironically, technology has turned back the clock from disinterested enjoyment of high and popular art to a primitive culture of crude, grasping self-interest. And yet these drastic transformations are difficult to perceive and make sense of. The Internet is a parallel universe that rarely intersects with other spheres of life outside its defensive parameters.

Here is John Battelle, a co-founder of *Wired* magazine, in his book, *The Search: How Google and Its Rivals Rewrote the Rules of Business and Transformed Our Culture.* Like Toffler and Gladwell, Battelle is all for bringing leisure time into the marketplace:

> On the Internet, it can be argued, all intent is commercial in one way or another, for your very attention is valuable to someone, even if you're simply researching your grandmother's genealogy, or reading up on a rare species of dolphin. Chances are you'll see plenty of advertisements along the way, and those links are the gold from which search companies spin their fabled profits.

Battelle wants to press home the importance of multiple searches to advertisers. He uses the following quotation to make his point:

Thorstein Veblen, the early-twentieth-century thinker who coined the term "conspicuous consumption," once quipped, "The outcome of any serious research can only be to make two questions grow where only one grew before" . . . In fact, Pew research shows that the average number of searches per visit to an engine [that is, a search engine, like Google] is nearly five . . . This copious diversity drives not only the complexity of the search itself, but also the robustness of the advertising model that supports it.

But Veblen was talking about the humanistic value of research, not the commercial value of a "search"! He was saying that the world was ultimately mysterious and unfathomable, and that therefore the quest for knowledge had no terminus—that the disinterested, endless quest for knowledge was an end in itself. Battelle can only understand Veblen in the context of commerce and the Web.

Which context is often so unreal, yet so confident in its unreality, that it has the very real effect of making any criticism of it seem absurd.

That's what Alice Mathias, a senior at Dartmouth College, discovered. On a blog in the *New York Times* called "The Graduates: Eight College Seniors Face the Future," Mathias contributed a dry, witty, yet openhearted column titled "Love in the Digital Age." She concluded it like this:

For example, Dartmouth students have recently had to deal with the construction of the Web site boredatbaker.com (which has cousins at the other Ivies, the Massachusetts Institute of Technology, New York University and

Stanford). Intended as a community tool, this Web site has mutated into a forum for the anonymous publication of very personal attacks on students who must try their best not to be emotionally affected when people publicly question their sexuality, comment on their physical appearance and speculate about their value as humans.

In anonymous Internet attacks, people can say things they would never mention aloud while looking their target in the eye. No one need take any personal responsibility. The victims of these unfortunate manifestations of free speech must suspend their emotions and try to trust that people around them (including love interests) aren't the ones who are writing or consuming this stuff. The safest thing to do in our boredatbaker-shadowed community is to be emotionally isolated from everyone until graduation brings escape.

College students used to be the active arm of society's conscience. The ones, like Mathias, with the most sensitive consciences often protested war, racial bias, inequitable social policies. If an instance of corruption or injustice occurred in the town or city where they went to school, they often took to the streets to demonstrate or to march with the local townspeople or to stand on a picket line. Or maybe they just edited a mordantly honest literary magazine. Now they tremble helplessly before the Internet's Alice-in-Wonderland, truth-eliding, boundary-busting juggernaut.

What can they do? The language of protest college students once used—democracy, freedom, power to the people, revolution—has been taken over by the very forces that are invading and bruising their inner lives. The people who run boredat baker.com would no doubt respond to criticism of their anonymous character assassinations by echoing Lawrence Lessig, Jay Rosen, and others and crying "free speech" and "democracy" and "don't fight the future." Graduation probably won't bring escape, either. At Gawker.com, a Manhattan-based Web site that makes random attacks on media figures, a site run by people you've never heard of—who might just as well be anonymous—you even have the opportunity to buy the official Gawker T-shirt, which has the word "Douché," referring to a favorite Gawker insult, printed on the front. Incredibly, the high-school stigma of unpopularity has become so great that the accomplished adults of the New York media world live in fear of this adolescent silliness.

In this upside-down new world, student rebellion would have the appearance of reactionary resentment. But then, in this new upside-down world, politically active students appear in long threads on political blogs as "hits" rather than as real bodies protesting in the streets.

8

Being There

BY NOW, IT'S PROBABLY becoming clear that when Internet boosters speak ringingly about "the many wresting power from the few," as *Time* put it, what they usually mean is finding a different way for the same old few to bring in many new customers.

When Amazon.com invites people to "review" the books it is selling—when it invites people to become "producers"—it is flattering egos, building trust, and opening wallets and purse strings. When news organizations invite readers to comment on articles and even suggest subjects to write about, they are creating—or so they hope—a whole new generation of readers who will pay to read their own comments under a (previously) prestigious masthead and to enjoy the effects of their "input."

There is one obstruction, however, to the Internet's aspiration to make every corner of social life accessible to anyone with a modem. Expertise. That's why you never hear about the Internet causing a "revolution" in law or medicine, or in electrical contracting, for that matter. Professions and trades require training. You could not have the equivalent of Jay Rosen creating "citizen heart surgeons."

Instead, the Internet boosters' target is culture, the realm of "creativity." Their inspiration has been to professionalize "self-expression" and to put it on the marketplace alongside every other skill. Not everyone can become a doctor—but everyone knows how to express himself. We all have a Ph.D., as it were, in our own lives. Our opinions and judgments, feelings and perceptions are our own field of expertise. When journalists or scholars authoritatively express themselves on any aspect of life, they are foolishly presuming an exclusive claim on a subject that we have mastered just fine for ourselves, thank you.

Since culture's aim is always to represent the human, simply being human has now become sufficient qualification for engaging in cultural expression. You don't have to be funny to be a comedian; all you have to do is present yourself as a comedian and insist that you are making jokes. You don't have to possess a perceptive, synthesizing, verbally nimble mind to be a journalist; all you have to do is present yourself as a journalist and insist—on your blog, for example—that you are doing journalism. The result is often a crude caricature of egalitarianism, in which more and more people, having asserted themselves as one type of culture maker or another, suddenly realize that a professional identity requires a professional skill and find themselves at a loss to practice what they claim to be. And so they end up merely repeating their right to be who they want to be, an incessant declaration of self that often takes the form of mockery or rage directed against privileged elites perceived to be standing in the majority's way. (The proclamation of life itself as a profession—the elevation of biology over talent and craft—is probably why so much of Web culture consists of adolescent jokes and taunts having to do with the body—"you smell like ass" is a favorite.)

Yet a fundamental question presents itself: What is privileged or elite about mastering a skill, or embodying an innate excellence in a craft, and building a life out of that? That is one powerful way in which disadvantaged people leap over social barriers. Democracy is what makes such transformation possible. What the new, crude egalitarianism is doing, in the name of democracy, is allowing the strongest assertion to edge out the most conscientious talent.

An example of this antidemocratic egalitarianism is the dance of triumph performed by numerous literary blogs when they heard the news that the *L.A. Times* and other papers were abolishing their book review sections. The happy blogs heralded what they hoped would be the imminent arrival of a new age where literary culture would be in the hands of literary bloggers rather than in the care of professional editors working for established institutions. "No great loss," wrote the blogger who runs—ironically—a blog called Literature Is Not Dead. "Newspaper book reviews suck. They are horrible." The Millions blog proclaimed: "There is a big audience for online book coverage, and online allows the discussion of books to break out of the 'review' mold that may be contributing to the decline in the viability of newspaper book sections."

But what the emboldened bloggers never stopped to consider is that culture is a vulnerable phenomenon. Its critical aspect makes it as dispensable to entrenched interests as it is indispensable to the lone individual. Culture needs authoritative institutions like a powerful newspaper; it needs them both to protect its critical, independent spirit and to make sure that culture's voices get heard in the louder din of more powerful economic and political entities. With all its various centers of power, and checks and balances, a newspaper is a lot less biased—for all its commercial pressures—and a lot less susceptible to hostile influences than the unchecked ego and will of a single blogger. The checks that blogs provide on the institutional authority of influential newspapers have a place, but a place as part of a larger context. Ironically, in their attempts at being iconoclastic and attacking big media (although applying that term to a book review section seems absurd), the bloggers are playing into the hands of political and financial forces that want nothing more than to see the critical, scrutinizing media disappear.

Having made living a life itself a type of professional skill, the Internet has produced another effect. It has created a universal impatience with authority, with any kind of superiority conferred by excellence or expertise. The pastiches of famous people performed by *American Idol*'s contestants are one manifestation of that impatience. So are YouTube's endless mashups deriding or travestying celebrated works of entertainment or art.

It's not clear what the popular mash-up of Fellini's *8½* and Curtis Hanson's *8 Mile*, starring Eminem, means besides its creator's desire to quickly emulate both films—under the pretext of making something new—in lieu of patiently making one just as good as either. Mash-ups depend on audience recognition of what is being combined and parodied. But it's hard to reframe the originals when the originals' expressive power, such as it is, is being so carefully maintained—as in, for example, remix artist Danger Mouse's *The Grey Album,* a mash-up of the Beatles' *White Album* and rapper Jay-Z's *The Black Album.* It's diverting, but you find yourself listening intently to the originals underneath the attempt at fusion. Effective montage and especially collage—the montage of the great dadaist Hannah Höch, for example, and the collage of Kurt Schwitters—utterly submerge their original fragments in the newly created whole. However, most mash-ups are sheepish imitations disguised as bold new creations or attacks. (Danger Mouse indeed.) They put you in mind of Christopher Lasch's definition of the clinical narcissist (quoted in chapter 3) as someone "whose sense of self depends on the validation of others whom he nevertheless degrades."

Combined with the habit of living vicariously instilled in us by watching television and movies, our impatience with anyone higher than us is one of the fuels of Internet interactivity. The commenters on blogs, the mash-up artists, the reviewers on Amazon, the "citizen journalists"—they are all reaching, seizing, and trying to reshape the public images of people who seem to inhabit exclusive niches. Nowhere is this more rampant than on Wikipedia, the online encyclopedia.

Created in 2001, Wikipedia is an encyclopedia with a novel premise. Anyone can create or edit its articles, whether the person is a respected university professor or a freshman in high school. Contributors are not even required to use their own names. Yes, that's right. There is now an online encyclopedia that is created and edited by anonymous people who are free to misrepresent historical facts and malign living people. Sometimes these outrages are discovered and corrected right away, sometimes they are discovered and corrected after days, weeks, or months, and sometimes they are never discovered or corrected.

By now, the tales of mistakenly or deliberately false entries in Wikipedia are legion. A typical instance is the case of John Seigenthaler Sr., a journalist whose entry wrongly claimed that "he was thought to have been directly involved in the Kennedy assassinations of both John and his brother, Bobby." That terrible error stayed in the article about Seigenthaler for four months, during which time it was repeated on other widely read "reference" sites throughout the Internet.

A twenty-four-year-old named Ryan Jordan was caught masquerading on Wikipedia as a tenured professor of religion. He used the pseudonym Essjay and aroused suspicion when readers began to wonder why a professor of religion was meticulously revising the encyclopedia's article on pop star Justin Timberlake. By then, Jordan had created or edited hundreds of articles. He had even been made an "administrator" and was part of Wikipedia's trusted inner circle of editors.

Wikipedia calls these instances of untruth "vandalism," as if the encyclopedia were experiencing an onslaught of invaders from beyond its boundaries. But the "vandals" are part of the Wikipedia enterprise, just as Jordan was. They've been invited to participate in its creation just like every other "Wikipedian." They avail themselves of the same mode of access and the same anonymity as everyone else who is creating and editing articles. Jimmy Wales, Wikipedia's founder, was caught misrepresenting facts in his own biographical article, which he edited to exclude the contributions made to Wikipedia by a former business partner. For a while, at the top of its entry on Douglas Rushkoff,

Wikipedia had posted this warning: "THIS ARTICLE OR SECTION IS WRITTEN LIKE AN ADVERTISEMENT."

In tyrannical regimes, you could denounce anyone to the secret police: a professional or romantic rival, or someone you simply bore a grudge against. Now in America, in the name of the marketplace, you have similar opportunities, *mutatis mutandis*. Wales talks the usual egalitarian talk. But he didn't start out as a thinker, or a writer, or as any kind of disinterested humanist. Like so many other people in the 2.0 cuckoo's nest, he started out as a businessman. He made his money trading bonds and operating a "dot.com erotic search engine" called Bomis. At least that's what his Wikipedia entry says today.

A SIMPLE QUESTION

Click on the "talk page" for the disputed entry for Marlon Brando in Wikipedia, and you get the following discussion among Wikipedia contributors:

> Brando's longtime hatred of Presley apparently went back to 1957 when they met in a restaurant and the 5'8" actor realized he was in the company of someone who was younger, taller, more handsome, more popular and infinitely more talented than he ever could be.

> What does that have to do with anything? And how can you prove this? *:: ehmjay* 22:53, 5 July 2006 (UTC)

> That's a matter of opinion. Elvis was a musician ... Brando was an actor. Elvis is considered by many to be the

king of rock and roll. Brando is considered to be one of the finest actors of all time—however very eccentric. He is hardly untalented. He could act, Elvis could not—not many people would dispute that. I'm not sure about the mentally unfit to serve in WWII, and just because Elvis did doesn't make him a hero . . . especially to non-Americans like myself. .:: *ehmjay* 18:00, 6 July 2006 (UTC)

Elvis was an actor AND a musician. Ok, his movies weren't as great as Bing Crosby's, but they were still a lot better than Wacko Jacko's paltry offerings.

The article itself is nearly as semiliterate. About Brando's outsider image, you read the following: "All the rebel culture that included motorcycle, leather jackets, jeans and the whole rebel image, that inspired generations of rebels, came thanks to the movie *The Wild One* and Brando's own unique image and character."

Tonal slants are a lot harder to correct than factual errors. The article about the great American orator Henry Ward Beecher describes his wife as being "unloved." The reference cited for that "fact" is a book review by the scholar Michael Kazin, in which Kazin refers fleetingly to "the steadfast loyalty of Beecher's unloved wife." But the review itself does not cite any factual evidence for such a judgment. Who knew what Kazin was thinking when he wrote that, or how he arrived at that judgment?

In *The Columbia Encyclopedia*, Beecher's entry describes only the consequential, demonstrable, public facts of his life, not personal details that are subject to infinite interpretation.

Wikipedia's particular innovation is to place the most subjective interpretations of a figure's private life right next to the demonstrable public facts. It's the first encyclopedia to include gossip in its articles. It's also the first encyclopedia to include the biographies of ordinary living people—like poor Mr. Seigenthaler, history's most accomplished assassin. (Which brings gossip dangerously close to libel.) But then, the capacity to embellish famous historical figures with gossip affords greater emotional involvement to Wikipedia's contributors. The effect is to create a familiar, memoir-like, inhabitable first-person-type experience. A participatory experience.

Wikipedia's "talk" pages are frequently interminable bursts of angry back-and-forth between "volunteer" editors and contributors, some of whom are as young as fifteen. Because articles exist on various levels of contestation, entries are preceded by various advisories: "This article or section needs a complete rewrite for the reasons listed on the talk page"; "This article or section does not adequately cite its reference sources"; "The factual accuracy of this article is disputed"; "This article may require cleanup to meet Wikipedia's quality standards"; "This article documents a current event. Information may change rapidly as the event progresses"; "Editing of this article by unregistered or newly registered users is currently disabled"; "This page is currently protected editing until disputes have been resolved." Wikipedia might say that these warnings are proof of the collaborative encyclopedia's commitment to fairness and accuracy. But a reader could well ask what the point is of an encyclopedia in which meaning and value are constantly shifting, being challenged, disproved, or exposed as the fraudulent product of ulterior motives.

Change happens fast in America. Claims of newness are intimidating, and the fear of being left behind is threatening. The result is that you suddenly find yourself meekly asking how a recent phenomenon can be fixed or improved, rather than asking the more fundamental question: Why is it here at all? In the face of all this absurdity, which fifteen years ago would have been the plot of a science-fiction novel, you have to step back and take stock.

So why does Wikipedia exist? If you ask its promoters the question, they'll look at you as though you were wearing a loincloth and carrying a club. It is "democratizing knowledge," they'll mechanically recite. If you ask them what they mean by that, they'll automatically respond that the Wikipedians are "wresting power from the few" who compose standard encyclopedias like *Britannica* and empowering "the many."

If you persist, and say that democracy produced *Britannica*, and that someone is more free to disagree with its stable articles than with "wikied" articles that lurch from one prejudice to another, from one incoherence to another, they'll recite: "More information." If you argue that Wikipedia's misinformation is not the same thing as information, they'll recite: "Decentralization" and "Freedom." If you say that *Britannica*, though written by committees of academic experts, sticks to the broad, demonstrable, public facts and doesn't impose a narrow psychological and emotional speculation on its subjects; if you say that reference works like *Britannica* are well written and tonally neutral and that these qualities are boons to intellectual freedom; if you say that *Britannica*'s articles are so general and careful that there is little to contest in them—if you point all this out and add that in many parts of the developed world, more people have access to

Britannica at their local library than to the Internet, and then you ask why the subjective chaos of Wikipedia is necessary, they'll throw up their hands. "It's convenient!" they'll say. "Duh!"

INFORMATION IS POWERLESSNESS

"Convenience" is also the rote answer to another fundamental question: Why does anyone not employed in the news media need a constant flow of news and information? One of the Internet boosters' proudest claims is that the Internet can deliver the news to its users with unprecedented immediacy. If someone gets shot in a supermarket parking lot in Flagstaff, Arizona, an Internet user in New Jersey will know about it hours, maybe even days before someone who depends on his local evening news. But who really needs to know that? Who needs to assimilate the unrelenting reams of information directed at us twenty-four hours a day?

A friend—a journalist, as it happens—recently sent me an e-mail describing a trip she and her family took to George Washington University, where her son was thinking of going to college:

> We made our first college visit yesterday, to GW . . . Our tour of the grounds did not include a trip to any library or bookstore, but we were taken to the state-of-the-art lobby of the business-school building, where four oversized flat screens tuned to four different stations flicker with the latest headlines, as if anyone could ingest that much informa-

tion at once. It made me feel v. sad—what sort of bookless world are my children heading into?

Well, no one can ingest so much information at once. Yet, again, if you push against an Internet enthusiast's claims that the Internet delivers news faster than the speed of light, he will answer your question with the tautological reiteration of his claim. Information is good because information is good. Democracy depends on information and on full access to information, he will tell you. An informed citizenry is an empowered citizenry. For too long, the elite media outlets controlled access to information. The Internet has thrown those exclusive and excluding doors wide open. And on and on.

The Internet does indeed have achievements in the news business. It has forced the traditional news outlets to seek out more and more trivial news, in order to compete with the Internet. And it has engorged the "old" media with streams of useless information.

The latter development is yet another consequential creation of a new value that thrives behind the mask of an old one. For what this new religion of information has done is to pretend that information now has the power of knowledge. In the process, knowledge has been devalued into information.

Now, information is a good thing. In situations of emergency or crisis, it is a vitally good thing. But information is composed of facts with which one has only recently become acquainted, facts that have value because they are communicable entities that many people want to possess. You desire knowledge for its own sake, not for the sake of knowing what someone else knows, or for the sake of being able to pass it on to someone else. Knowledge guarantees your autonomy. Information gets you thinking like everyone else who is absorbing the same information.

To put it another way: knowledge means you understand a subject, its causes and consequences, its history and development, its relationship to some fundamental aspect of life. But you can possess a lot of information about something without understanding it. An excess of information can even disable knowledge; it can unmoor the mind from its surroundings by breaking up its surroundings into meaningless data. Distraction has the obvious effect of driving out reflection, but because we are reading or watching the "news" rather than enjoying a diversion, we feel serious and undistracted. Never mind that the news has often been more diverting than the most absorbing diversions, and now more than ever. The more we concentrate on the news, the more distracted we are.

Like John Battelle's miscomprehension of the disinterested Veblen, the Internet has no interest in knowledge for its own sake. It prizes information because, unlike knowledge, information has exchange value on the market. Nobody is going to pay you for explaining what Epictetus or Montaigne had to say about suffering. Timeliness and its ability to serve our practical interest are what determine the value of information. But Epictetus's abstract musings are neither "pegged" to the moment nor able to change our worldly situation. Therefore, they are not information. Unless, of course, Al Gore dedicates his next book about the environment "to the work and legacy of Epictetus." Then the ancient Stoic becomes valuable in the marketplace.

For once a few people start talking about something that has been on the airwaves, more and more people will want to pay to know as much about it as they can. Commentary and analysis of the news event slice it up into ever more exclusive news niches, creating more markets and more demand.

Remember elementary school, when all the kids were talking about a TV show they saw the previous night and you couldn't participate in the conversation because your parents made you go to bed before it was on? The dynamics of news "buzz" are like that. If everyone is standing around the water cooler talking about the shifting incarnations of the latest buzz—a shrink said Don Imus was a sociopath on *Larry King*! Imus's lawyer said at a news conference that he was going into therapy, it was on CNN! MSNBC has pictures of Imus looking silly on the street!—and you're still on last month's buzz—Obama went to an Islamic school!—you're going to feel like you're still listening to a Walkman instead of an iPod. You're going to feel like "history," or like a "dinosaur," or "old."

By possessing the latest news, the most recent buzz, we feel younger than the suddenly old news, than the superseded last buzz. The manic news cycle, in which the hottest, newest stories immediately give way to hotter, newer stories, gives its audience the illusion that they and the world they live in are ageless. Information has become fashion cycles for the mind.

Information, we are told again and again these days, is the guarantor of a free society. But this simply is not true. Modern dictatorships also have their streams of information. Not all of it is propaganda, either. The subjects of tyrannies get relentless dispatches on the state of the world and of life on the farm or collective; human interest stories galore; commentary on trade and economics. Slanted? Of course it is. But so is much of our news, pegged as it is to what happens to be the hot movie, or the hot TV show, or the previously hot news story of the moment. Not to mention advertising.

As for more substantial news, you could have disclosures of political corruption or social injustice being broadcast throughout the day, yet if you lacked the ethical and historical bearings to make sense of them, they would have no beneficial effect on your life or anyone else's. Many Germans had information about the slave labor and the concentration camps during the 1940s, but because the entire society had lost its ethical and historical bearings, such terrible revelations roused no serious protest. Americans throughout the country had information about blacks being tortured and killed in the American South for decades after Reconstruction. But it wasn't until brave leaders and writers changed the nation's ethical and historical framework that the era of civil rights began. It is knowledge that gives us our ethical and historical ballast, and knowledge also brings the critical detachment necessary to arrive at that humane stability. Critical detachment, not the multiple diversions and distractions of information, is the guarantor of a free society.

Under the influence of the Internet, however, knowledge is withering away into information. Wikipedia, with its video-game-like mode of participation, and with its mountains of trivial factoids, of shifting mounds of gossip, of inane personal details, is knowledge in the process of becoming information.

At the same time, consumer participation in the creation of the news is information crumbling into particles of incoherence. The grainy, jumpy cellphone video of people advancing carefully, and then running, across Virginia Tech's campus as Cho Seung-Hui committed his hideous murders was empty of even the most superficial newsy meaning. You could barely see the people; the setting was almost impossible to make out. This was not "information" by any stretch of the imagination. What appeal the footage did have was an inhabitable, first-person quality of being captured by someone (like you, the viewer) who was not in the situation but was emotionally caught up by it— the jumpy camera reproduced your own fascinated, horrified response while watching. It also flattered all the videobloggers who were tuned in to the news that evening.

The weeks and weeks of petty disclosures and inane analysis that followed the Virginia Tech massacre were also meaningless—more versions of information masquerading as knowledge, as psychologists offered their research-based "findings." No one needed them to understand the emotional consequences of what had happened, or to grasp what it perhaps said about the American psyche, or to apprehend its social ramifications. It was collective human knowledge—that is, experience refined into consciousness by thought and reflection—that, in the end, conferred meaning on senseless, bloody facts.

Such knowledge illuminates the hidden relations among events, and the degrees of value between events. It's what enabled some people to turn away from the news in disgust when psychological analysis of Cho's motives for slaughtering gave way to psychological analysis of Alec Baldwin's motives for leaving a mean message for his eleven-year-old daughter on her answering machine. They found the easy segue from tragedy into trivia vertiginous. They were guided by their critical detachment. But the sources of critical detachment are drying up, as book supplements disappear from newspapers and what passes for critical thinking in the more intellectually lively magazines gives way to the Internet's emphasis on cuteness, novelty, buzz, and pursuit of the "viral." By surrendering to the Internet's ideology of information, the traditional print outlets have started to remove the independent spaces where people used to be able to stand, detached from the hectic axial lines of self-interest, and make sense of what was happening around them, and of all the torrents of information rushing toward them.

I'm not talking about a dearth of long, contemplative articles, or of what is known in journalism as "the think piece." These are often exercises in forced, old-fashioned "seriousness"—the Restoration Hardware of reflection. No, when I say critical distance, I mean articles of any length written in a spirit of skeptical detachment and adversarial engagement.

But we are living in a popularity culture, where being liked is the supreme value. Therefore, few people write critically about anything anymore. Instead of criticism, the air brims with mockery and sarcasm—think of Jon Stewart, Stephen Colbert, and Sacha Baron Cohen. They can be very funny. Mockery and sarcasm, though, merely take information, crumple it up into a ball, and throw it back whence it came. Trapped in the vicious circles of information, Stewart and Colbert rely on the news for their derision of the news. Yet satire that depends on information for its effect is just another mode of information. As such, it possesses the same market value as information. It is swayed by the same specter of popularity.

In September 2006, a perceptive article appeared in the *New York Times Magazine* called "My Satirical Self." The author,

Wyatt Mason, argued that social criticism was now mostly in the hands of the comedians and that their humor was characterized by a tone which was "so sarcastic, so ironic, so sardonic." He singled out Stewart and Colbert especially.

Mason celebrated the new tone. He tried to trace it all the way back through Mark Twain and Swift to the Roman satirist Juvenal, though he ended up conceding that contemporary humor had more cynicism and sarcasm than what he liked to think were its satirical precursors. He concluded his essay with an acute insight. After characterizing the rhetorical tone of President George Bush—our contemporary mockers' standard subject—as "consistently condescending," he wrote:

> That tone—carelessly sarcastic, thoughtlessly ironic, indiscriminately sardonic—that is the very one you now find everywhere. Bush is us; Bush is me . . . It makes me wonder what happens when the language of argument and the language of ridicule become the same, when the address of a potentate is voiced no more soberly than the goofings of some rube.

What happens when the language of argument and the language of ridicule become the same? It's an essential thing to wonder and worry about. What Mason might well have been asking was: How can we transform the disabling waves of information into islands of critical detachment, instead of merely turning them inside out by means of mockery and ridicule?

The striking element of Mason's essay was its disproportionately adversarial ending. This conclusion of an article that celebrated the contemporary style of derision should have been the premise of an article that critically exposed much of contemporary humor's complicity with the status quo. Perhaps Mason did not want to risk the cascade of obloquy that would have fallen on him from the popularity-driven blogosphere if he had developed an argument about, say, the similarity between the contemptuous sarcasm of sensationally popular Stephen Colbert and the contemptuous sarcasm of sensationally unpopular George W. Bush.

Who could blame Mason for his caution, given the deafening clamor of mockery, taunting, and rage that is all around us? The deafening clamor of tons upon tons of information being chewed up and spat derisively out. The sound of the blogosphere.

9

The Emperor's New Modem

THERE ARE CURRENTLY ABOUT seventy million blogs in existence, with between forty thousand and fifty thousand being created every day. There are political blogs, and cultural blogs, and personal blogs, blogs devoted to a particular profession, blogs for expectant mothers, blogs for martial arts competitors, blogs for poets, photographers, and sex addicts. What's now called the blogosphere truly is a world unto itself.

Seventy million people are continuously engaged in presenting their general reflections and private thoughts in public, for other people. For the first time in history, individuals can, easily and directly, without the slightest mediating conditions, express themselves to the vast public on the largest scale imaginable. They can choose to do this under their own name or anonymously, and there are no limits on what they may express. A blog is accountable to no one, and bloggers may manipulate their "archives" through revision or deletion. Obviously, this new world has its pathological aspects.

Yet the science-fiction-like dystopian side of the blogosphere never gets commented on at length. The culture wars may rage, bouncing from one symbolic event to another; politics may be bitterly polarized; the American media may thrive on antagonism, scandal, gotcha exposés, and contrarian thinking in various degrees—but the blogosphere gets nary a critical paw laid on it.

Part of the immunity to criticism lies in the fact that the blogosphere has become the proving ground for the Internet boosters' claims of democracy and anti-elitism. But there are more concrete reasons. Blogs started to take off in 1994, at the height of dot-com prosperity—blogs and the soaring economy are almost synonymous. The 1990s were also the moment when commercial society began to focus on the youth market with unprecedented fervor—one of the fathers of the blogosphere was a student at Swarthmore College named Justin Hall, who kept an online diary for eleven years.

This chapter takes up bloggers—political, cultural, or personal—who see themselves as shaping the public discourse in some way, whether by commenting on the continuous streams of news or by trying to provide their own information. About this strange new culture, just about everyone who still has a professional or personal stake in pre-Internet culture will secretly confide to you the following observations:

OPEN SECRET NUMBER ONE: Bloggers' ability to revise or erase their writing without leaving any trace of the original post is the very antithesis of their claims of freedom and access and choice. The freedom and access and choice are theirs, not their readers'.

OPEN SECRET NUMBER TWO: The individual news blogger's lack of an institution's ethical framework encourages the mutation of rumor into fact. Examples run to the hundreds, even thousands. Here are a few of the most colorful or consequential: In February 2004, the blogger Matt Drudge falsely claimed that John Kerry had had an affair with an intern on Capitol Hill who then fled to Africa. After the tsunami hit Indonesia in December 2004, the Internet was teeming with photographs and video clips of the event that proved to be false. According to the *L.A. Times,* a rumor about a North Korean warhead still thrives on certain conservative blogs. A blog's false report that one of the traders at Knight Trading Group Inc. had been arrested made the company's stock plunge by 14 percent. A Manhattan Web site dedicated to slandering young members of New York's high society nearly destroyed the reputations of several people until the anonymous blog was threatened with a lawsuit for libel.

OPEN SECRET NUMBER THREE: Lust for recognition rules the blogosphere. As Robert Scoble and Shel Israel put it in *Naked Conversations: How Blogs Are Changing the Way Businesses Talk with Customers:* "Blogging turns out to be the best way to secure a high Google ranking . . . Blogs get updated all the time, while most web sites do not, so blogs get more search engine attention." Blogs are in the vanguard of the popularity culture. *They must sound more like everyone else than anyone else is able to sound like everyone else.* On any given day, the political and gossip blogs move in lockstep from one hot topic to the next. What gets attention is the most outrageous variation on what everyone is talking about. That gets the most links, and the most links get the most page views, and the most page views win the highest Google ranking. Traditional media outlets have divided the business side from the editorial side. Bloggers, who are pro-sumers par excellence, are in the business of selling their only product, which is themselves.

OPEN SECRET NUMBER FOUR: The most prominent bloggers, despite their cries of the "mainstream" media's elitism, hubris, bias, exclusion, and complicity with the powers that be, rush to join the mainstream media as soon as it beckons. In fact, since the blogosphere represents mass opinion galvanized by the promise of approval and recognition, it is more mainstream than the so-called mainstream media ever were.

OPEN SECRET NUMBER FIVE: Established journalists have skillfully used their own blogs, as well as the rhetoric of Internet populism and dissent, to assimilate, tame, and edge out bloggers who threaten their elite perches.

OPEN SECRET NUMBER SIX: The blogosphere's democratic revolution excludes vast numbers of people too poor to invest the money in computers and software, as well as people who don't have access to training in the use of computers. The most popular and prestigious bloggers comprise an elite technocracy. They are almost all, to a man and woman, white and middle- to upper-middle-class.

OPEN SECRET NUMBER SEVEN: Big media have embraced the blogosphere not in the name of higher democratic values but because they fear becoming the object of the blogosphere's un-constrained derision. Being publicly insulted is now worse than being called professionally incompetent. Being repeatedly called a "wanker" or an "assclown"—two favorite blogospheric taunts—now amounts to a social stigma. That's what happens when popularity replaces excellence as the sole criterion of success.

OPEN SECRET NUMBER EIGHT: Big media have embraced the blogosphere not in the name of higher democratic values but because going online will save newspapers and magazines tens of millions of dollars in production overhead and mailing costs. It used to be that going down-market made news outlets vulnerable to charges of "dumbing down"; it also lost them discriminating readers. In this sense, the blogosphere is big media's Seventh Cavalry. Newspapers and magazines can continue to cut costs, please shareholders, and go down-market, but now in the name of freedom and equality for all. Going online doesn't make money in journalism—*Slate,* the most successful online magazine, has never turned a profit. Going online saves money. At a time when shareholders aren't content with steady profitability, but demand constant growth, media outlets need to save all the money they can.

FIVE OPEN SUPERSECRETS

1. Not everyone has something meaningful to say.
2. Few people have anything original to say.
3. Only a handful of people know how to write well.
4. Most people will do almost anything to be liked.
5. "Customers" are always right, but "people" aren't.

It bears repeating that just fifteen years ago, blogospheric excesses would have been considered a democratic crisis. Fifteen years ago the following sentence describing the inevitability of blogs—it appeared in *Fortune* magazine—would have been derided as sounding like the ultimatum of a mobster who tells the owner of a small business to accept "protection" or else: "Freewheeling bloggers can boost your product—or destroy it. Either way, they've become a force business can't afford to ignore." Now the blogosphere's drags on fairness, honesty, and accuracy are accepted as an immutable condition, a set of trade-offs that have to be made for the sake of democracy, anti-elitism, true dissent, and greater access to information. It follows, then, that any criticism of the blogosphere is antidemocratic, elitist, protective of the status quo, and a form of censorship.

But if you are stigmatized as being elitist and antidemocratic—not to mention prehistoric—every time you criticize the Internet, when is it ever possible to criticize the Internet without being called elitist and antidemocratic? (Not to mention prehistoric?)

TREAD ON ME

The open secrets of blogospheric nightmare are not entirely secret. They are sometimes "conscientiously" alluded to by journalists, who then prudently let the subject drop. The *Time* cover story celebrating the average Internet user as "Person of the Year" paused to add that "Web 2.0 harnesses the stupidity of crowds as well as its wisdom. Some of the comments on

YouTube make you weep for the future of humanity just for the spelling alone, never mind the obscenity and the naked hatred." As if the facile equivalence between bad spelling and naked hatred were not enough to cancel out the article's seeming concern, the writer concluded: "But that's what makes all this interesting."

Yet since when is "naked hatred" merely "interesting"? As for the "stupidity of crowds," that phrase is virtually a synonym for the most destructive kind of politics. And all the vitriol is hardly just on YouTube, but *Time*'s writer apparently did not want to alienate more of the blogosphere than he felt he had to.

David Carr, who blogs the Oscars every year for the *New York Times*, is acutely aware of the blogosphere's dangers, and so he goes to even greater lengths of appeasement. "Like a lot of modern newspaper people," he told readers in January 2007, "I have a blog," as if not having one made you premodern. He continued:

> Independent bloggers can laugh all they want about the imperious posture of the mainstream media, but I and others at The Times have never been more in touch with readers' every robustly communicated whim than we are today. Not only do I hear what people are saying, but I also care.

Carr later deftly orchestrates a point about the effect of reader participation through blogs on the quality of the news:

> But at some point, ratings (which print journalists, unlike their television counterparts, have never had to contend

with) will start to impinge on news judgment. "You can bemoan the crass decision-making driving [*sic*] by ratings, but you can't really avoid the fact that page views are increasingly the coin of the realm," said Jim Warren, co-managing editor of The Chicago Tribune . . . "The best thing about the Web—you have so much information about how people use it—is also the worst thing," said Jim Brady, executive editor of Washingtonpost.com. "You can drive yourself crazy with that stuff. News judgment has to rule the day, and the home page cannot become a popularity contest."

But like the prudent *Time* writer, Carr ends his article with a ringing commitment to the brave new world. He writes radiantly, if a little archly, about his intimate relationship with a blogger named Mark Klein—this amounts to a *stretta di mano* to all those "modern" readers of blogs who hope to get their names mentioned in the *New York Times* along with Klein. Then he signs off as just another one of the millions of blogging guys: "I could go on, but the results of the awards by the Broadcast Film Critics just came in at 1:17 a.m., and I need to update my blog. No time like the present." A few months later, Carr was back, this time in the media column he writes for the "dead tree" (i.e., print) division of the newspaper. Summing up a column on the most recent White House Correspondents' Association dinner, he swerved into a bizarre non sequitur that had nothing to do with any part of the preceding article:

But the world outside the Beltway is becoming far less civil. Unlike elected Washington, the members of the

press are not facing term limits or an impending vote. But
if consumers continue to exercise their right to get news
when and where they feel like it, the press may eventually
get voted out all the same.

It's yet more evidence of the coercive atmosphere the Internet
boosters have created behind the pretense of greater freedom
that a gifted journalist like Carr could be reduced to writing
about the Internet in such a sheepish, ingratiating way. In such
an uncritical way. For a consumer exercising his right to get
news when and where he feels like it will probably depend on
biased outlets; mediocre or tendentious commentators; or "customized" sources that reflect back to him only what he wants
to hear. A "consumer's rights" to getting what he pays for are
hardly the same thing as an individual's rights to unbiased, rational, intelligent, and comprehensive news.

Make no mistake about it. Once Tofflerian ethics rule the information business and the "consumers" of news also become
the producers of news, "choice" will exist only for the sake of
choice. In the name of "full participation," unbiased, rational,
intelligent, and comprehensive news—news as a profession,
like the practice of law or medicine—will become less and less
available. Standards will get drowned out by the mass pressure
of universal access. For universal access requires that the news
deliver universally appealing items. Like demagogic politicians,
who appeal to appetite and emotion rather than reason, this will
be the age of demagogic journalism.

For proof, all you need to do is look at the online magazine
Slate (where I once happily served as art critic). Once the beneficiary of Microsoft largesse, *Slate* was sheltered from the pres-

sures of the marketplace. It was able to balance the best qualities of the Internet—independent-minded brevity and pith
poised atop speed and relevance—with the deliberation, accuracy, and reflectiveness of the best traditional journalism. But
Microsoft sold *Slate* to the Washington Post Company, which
soon made its new acquisition more receptive than *Slate* had
been to what consumers wanted.

As a result, penetrating political and cultural commentary
has given way to a pandering tone of adolescent caricature and
distraction. After all, articles that appeal to the mind strike people in different ways. Articles that are pitched to appetite and
sensation appeal to everybody. Here are a few recent headlines:
"Suckling Sucks," "The Heisman Sucks," "Beyoncé, Your Mix
Tape Sucks." One recent item delivered a roundup of "critical
buzz on David Halberstam's death." You get endless reports on
box-office economics ("In a crowded summer blockbuster season, someone's going to get hurt. Will it be Spider-Man?"); the
cutest angle on anything ("Whose Life Is Worth More, a Drug
Dealer or a Prostitute?"); and shrieking invective ("George
Tenet's Sniveling, Disgraceful New Book"). William Saletan, a
Slate writer who wrote a distinguished book about the culture
war over abortion, now serves up a regular column called
Human Nature. Some typical items: "Ten-Inch Duck";
"Vaginally De-livered"; "SpongeBoob"; "Digital Penetration";
"Global Farting"; "Why Banging Your Sister Is Icky."

The ensuing articles, almost wearily tacked on to the juicy
headlines, read like object lessons in appealing to the mob-self.
They are little études in creating Gladwell's notion of "sticky"
concepts that you just can't get out of your head. It is the journalistic equivalent of rabble-rousing.

EVERY MAN A KING

People like Carr and similar blogosphere boosters seem to think—or pretend to think—that "choice" and "consumer power" mean that all voices will be heard. But the Internet really is making news a "popularity contest": Witness the ubiquitous rankings in the online versions of newspapers of "Most recent e-mailed articles"; "Most recent blogged articles"; "Most popular articles." And as we all know from high school, anyone can be popular for fifteen minutes, if he stoops so low that he rises to a general allure.

To quote again from Scoble and Israel on blogging's special opportunity and appeal: "Our friends influence us more than any advertising or marketing campaign could ever dream of doing." For all their volatile outbursts, bloggers want most of all to make friends.

Much of those volatile outbursts are in fact performed for potential friends. The bloggers' bible is a Web site called Technorati that ranks the popularity of blogs in several different categories—page views, links, and such—on a continuous basis. It doesn't matter whether you are a political, literary, or ambitious personal blogger. You get the most links by blogging more noisily and more outrageously than everyone else on whatever buzzy topic everyone else is blogging about.

Newspapers, which report in the third person, break stories. Blogs, which comment in the first person, loudly obsess over them.

That's not, of course, how the Internet boosters regard it. As J. D. Lasica typically writes in the USC Annenberg *Online*

Journalism Review, the "guardians of old media" see the world like this: "We, the gatekeepers, gather the news and tell you what's important. Under this chiseled-in-stone setup, editors sort through and rank the news, controlling everything from the assignment of stories to their tone, slant and prominence on the page."

You really have to marvel at how the blogosphere has turned a quintessential product of democracy like the American newspaper into an obstruction to democracy. There's a reason why antidemocratic uprisings always seize the newspapers and the television and radio stations first. They are the arteries of a democracy. But in the eyes of much of the blogosphere, the mainstream media's inevitable shortcomings make it an organ of tyranny.

The effects of this transvaluation are personal as well as social. A humbly born individual could once use the qualities of expertise and excellence to breach exclusive enclaves in journalism. But in the name of full participation, those qualities are now associated with exclusion and insularity. As a barrier to the Internet's ideology of total access, merit has become a social liability.

There is no point of resistance, either. Not when the mainstream media themselves, cowering before shareholder voracity, are seizing on Internet prosumerism to cut costs and attract new markets even as they claim to cower before Internet voracity.

Jeff Jarvis is a prominent blogger who calls his blog BuzzMachine. In February 2005, after complaining that guardians of the old media like the *New York Times* had been ignoring what he called "the news judgment of the people" as represented by the blogosphere, Jarvis posted on his blog an open letter to Bill Keller, the executive editor of the *Times*:

I propose that we hold a one-day meeting of webloggers and Times editors and reporters to discover how the interests of both groups are aligned and how we can work together to improve news.

The problem, Mr. Keller, is that many of your reporters and editors hold citizens' media in obvious disdain that has become all too public in your pages . . . This means that they are slapping the public you would serve and, in fact, your own readers: people who still read news. This also means that they are missing stories.

Keller gallantly—and shrewdly—replied to Jarvis in two e-mails. The effect of Keller's gesture recalled those old cartoons by Edward Sorel depicting real meetings between historical figures, in particular the one that had Sarah Bernhardt fainting in Thomas Edison's arms as he took her around his laboratory. The swooning Jarvis not only immediately muted his criticism of the *Times*—but he accepted a consulting job with the newspaper! To the inviolable and autonomous news judgment of the people, we say, Sayonara.

As for the stories the newspapers are missing by "ignoring" the blogs, I go to BuzzMachine today. The first thing I see is a picture of Jarvis himself being interviewed on MSNBC, an image that is now the Web site's logo. The top story begins like this:

By the way, I've shocked a few reporters this week when I told them that I got far more editorial interference due to business interests while at Time Inc., as a critic for People and the founder of Entertainment Weekly, than I ever got as TV critic for TV Guide in News Corp.

The post goes on to detail Jarvis's courage in defying his corporate masters when he worked in the mainstream media. Jarvis's story is all about Jarvis. The front page of today's *New York Times* has, among others, articles about Florida changing the date for its presidential primary, diplomatic talks between the United States and Syria, the identification of a gene that puts people at risk for heart disease, and American public schools' disenchantment with laptop computers for students. I can't find anything about Keller. Not even his picture.

Pardon the ironic tone, but you see what I mean. When you accept pictures of the world framed in the third person, you are accepting a version of the world as a necessarily limited place that requires compromise and agreement to be understood. When, on the other hand, the only versions of the world you get are in the first person, reality seems to be whatever anyone wants it to be. A good newspaper gives you pictures of what other people are feeling. The first-person nature of blogs is like a firewall against sympathetic feeling.

This isn't to say that big media are not flawed, sometimes fatally, by hubris, complicity with the status quo, bias, greed, inaccuracy, and incompetence. But a newspaper, for example, is a permeable social situation that is dense with layers of differing perspectives, checks and balances, and standards that have evolved in tandem with the history of the institution and with the history of the society around it.

The choice of news is inevitably the result of subjectivity. But it's not a single, unified subjectivity. It's a loose collection of individual minds that, because of their qualities of difference from each other—differences in knowledge, talent, responsibility, status, authority, ego—occupy in the aggregate a space somewhere between subjectivity and objectivity.

Internet users generally, however, and bloggers especially inhabit an absolutely solitary space in which other people exist as stick figures filled out by the user's or blogger's conception of them. It is a personal space disguised as a social space. In the blogosphere, the ego operates unobstructed by other egos. That's why virulent hatred comes so easily, and why any response to it comes as a shock, and an outrage. Stick figures are not supposed to answer back. Not when they exist mostly in your head.

Epilogue: *Homo Interneticus*

LENIN ONCE SAID THAT imperialism is the final phase of capitalism. He was wrong. The final phase of capitalism, its bottomless final frontier, is the public unfolding of the private, individual psyche. It is a mode of being in which the individual has learned to retail his privacy as a public performance. As a public transaction.

A real social situation, even when people are not talking to one another, is full of faces and objects caught sight of, gestures seen, sounds heard that keep communication going. But these sights, sounds, gestures that keep communication going also serve as barriers to what you can express. You cannot be totally "yourself." There are too many concrete inhibitors. They keep drawing you outside yourself. They are not familiar, and you are not at ease with them. So many palpable unknowns and variables make you guarded. That is what it means to be in public.

And you yourself are there, physically present, visible. People can see where you begin and end. You cannot speak out of your own mental image of yourself, because your image of yourself—like everyone's image of himself—is of a person without limitations, and without end. So you have this private sense of yourself as boundless, yet there are the bounded people before you, who speak to you also as a bounded person. You have to meet them halfway.

Therefore you do not "express" yourself, which means that you are thinking only about yourself. You communicate, which means that you are thinking about yourself and about another person or other people, and about the environment, and the circumstances, and possibly the history you all share.

Once you are online, however, you don't have to be communicating with anyone in particular. Just being online means that you are communicating with everyone in general. Ads pop up, spam comes in. If you are a blogger, you are being linked to. Search engines pick up on what you post. E-mail waits to be opened. You are being asked questions. (Can Pretty Boy Save Boxing? Should Paris Go to Jail? Do You Know Your Credit Score?) Gradually, on e-mail, on your blog, on eBay, on JDate.com, by hook or by crook, the ghosts in your machine— other people—throng closer to you.

But they are not people. Sitting alone in front of your computer, online, you find yourself in a social situation that has been privatized—customized, you might say, for your own personal use. The social situation has been dissolved into your head. There are no physical reminders of where the other presences online begin and end. There are no concrete inhibitors. And because you are alone, without bounded people, or a definite environment, or delineated circumstances—because there is nothing to remind you that you yourself have limits—you can "express" yourself out of the infinite conception you have of yourself. No wonder "magical thinking" has become such a popular term.

The other people-like presences exist infinitely, too. The presence in a chat room, the blogger you are linking to, the words on a screen you are having a heated exchange with on-line, the man or woman you are seducing online—they are not, like the physical people you actually meet, finalities that mark the limit of where your desire can lead them. You are not re-sponding to the inflections of a voice, or to the fluctuating sig-nals of a real presence. Yet you are not writing, either, because you lack the autonomy and detachment that accompany the act of writing. The other presences online exist too much in your head to be authentic human presences; yet their phantasmal pressure on you as you interact with them makes you too re-sponsive to them to be genuinely writing.

Rather, the people you encounter on the Internet are half people and half building blocks for your fantasies. You yourself fill in their pixilated or digitized blanks. You yourself breathe life, like a god, into the ghosts in the machine in front of you. They are at the mercy of your mouse, of your interrupting, blocking, or disconnecting finger. They are at the mercy of what you want to do with them. "Forward her to a friend."

For there are no disinterested feelings on the Internet. You don't go online not knowing what you will find. You go online to write an e-mail, to open an e-mail, to search for specific infor-mation, to find the latest news, to buy something, to meet some-one, to converse about politics, to join in commenting on the topic of the second. You never enter the Internet as you would enter a park, or go onto the street, or browse through a bookstore. You don't go online to just go for a walk, not knowing what you'll find or who you'll meet. You go online to look for something. Everyone you meet online is looking for something, too. The Internet is the most deliberate, purposeful environment ever created.

On the Internet, an impulse is only seconds away from its gratification. Everyone you encounter online is an event in the force field of your impulses. The criterion for judging the worth of someone you engage with online is the degree of his or her availability to your will. As Al Cooper, a psychologist who studies the Internet, puts it: "There is little difference between thought and Internet-enabled action . . . The Internet provides immediate gratification that affects one's ability to inhibit previously managed drives and desires." In other words, the Internet creates the ideal consumer.

Such absolute liberation from constraints is why anonymity is so widespread on the Internet, and why everything on the Internet tends toward anonymity: the hidden solitude of sitting before the screen; the spectral half-person presence of being online; the sense of yourself and of other people as having no boundaries. After expertise, authority, and merit have fallen away as obstacles, identity remains the last barrier to the vicarious, acquisitive, totally accessing, fully participating Internet will. Anonymity, you might say, is the Internet's ultimate identity. If you are not who you are, you can be anyone you wish to be. The husband and father can be a fleet-footed single man; the political operative can assume an innocent nonpartisan voice; the blogger can throw his mediocrity into a tantrum of entitlement and tower over the famous novelist. Identity is the last inhibitor to "previously managed drives and desires." Once you can shift in and out of different lives, you can shift in and out of different markets.

Delbert Babenco is my alias in Second Life, a complete, self-contained virtual community. Over eight million people now belong to this online world. They hold jobs, create businesses, buy and sell land and other commodities, and build houses. Second Life has its own economy, its own marketplace, and its own currency of exchange called Linden dollars. A lot of people have begun selling their Linden dollars for real dollars and make a decent living in their virtual world. Book editors are even publishing novels based on the fictional experiences of Second Life inhabitants. "Delbert" is my own choice, by the way, but I picked "Babenco" out of Second Life's list of last names. You're allowed to choose your own first name, but you have to get your last name from Second Life. If you happen to see my avatar—tall, brown hair, black sneakers, and a red fedora—come over and say hi. Just "right click" on my avatar to get the essential information about me: my age, birthplace, goals in life. Well, Delbert's essential information, anyway.

In Second Life, work and play are fused into a seamless whole. You are diverting yourself and making money all at the same time. By participating in this world, you are consuming its goods and services, and by consuming, you are also helping Second Life to produce its fantasy business. Second Life is a Tofflerian paradise. In fact, being in Second Life is really like being on the Internet, which might just as well be called Second Life. "Your World, Your Imagination" goes Second Life's motto. Like the Internet, when you are in Second Life, you are not in a shared community. You are all alone—in your world, your imagination—together with other people who inhabit their separate worlds. "Connected" points of isolation.

Second Life is nothing compared to the most common Internet experience. Not only has the Internet made pornography so popular that it has driven pornographic movies and DVDs to the brink of extinction, but as in other areas of technology, like videos and camcorders, pornography is responsible for many of the Internet's advances.

Al Cooper, who edited *Sex and the Internet: A Guidebook for Clinicians*, writes that "a new sexual revolution has commenced with the staggering growth of computers and technology and the exponential expansion of the Internet." He adds that "even as the Web continues its exponential expansion, little is known about how this new medium is affecting sexuality in the United States and around the world." Mark Dery, a committed advocate of the transmogrification of the human through computer technology, happily agrees with Cooper's sense of a new sexual revolution. "The intertwisted themes," he writes in *Escape Velocity*, "of eroticized machines, technologically mediated sex, sex with technology, and the rerouting of carnal desires into high-tech orgies of destruction are woven through cyberculture." Unlike Cooper, though, Dery has no sense of a crisis in human relationships: "Sex with machines, together with dalliances conducted in virtual worlds, seems a seductive alternative in an age of AIDS, unwanted pregnancies, and sexually transmitted diseases." Cooper sees cybersex differently: "The Internet has become an outlet for unresolved sexual difficulties and unfocused sexual energy, including the acting out or repetition of traumatic experiences . . . It is easy to see how many might choose to hide from their real-world problems through increased or exclusive online interaction."

Pornography is no more exclusively about sex than the libido is. Pornography reflects a general way of relating to the world. It collapses public and private. It turns quintessential play into a type of labor. Because it involves the most primal appetite, it has a universal appeal and popularity. The consummate vicarious endeavor, it thrives on and guarantees anonymity. Pornography transfigures other people into instruments of your will, and it strips them of their own ego and desire, so that you can mentally manipulate them without fear of rejection or reprisal.

In a sense, pornography and technology are joined at the hip. They both transform the reality outside your head into means whose sole end is convenience. (Pleasure is convenience as physical sensation.) Technology is a blessing, and a miracle, but it will not lead you to other people as finalities, as ends in themselves existing outside your needs and desires.

We all need each other as means; we need each other as instruments of help, sustenance, and pleasure. But without experiencing each other as an end and not as a means, we will lose our freedom to live apart from other people's uses for us, and from ours for other people—the world around us will shrink to ourselves as the only reference point in the world. Yet the world will still be there, but we will no longer understand it. We will no longer be ready for it. Most dangerous of all, we will no longer be patient with it when it fails to fulfill our most superficial, and our most selfish, desires.

Technology without human and humane content is a round-trip with just one familiar destination. Commenting on the breakthrough of scientists at the MIT Touch Lab, who sent a sensation from Cambridge to a man in London wearing a glove attached to a computer, one radio announcer said:

> Inevitably, then, the fingertip touch the scientists experienced this month will blossom into a full-blown body suit. In fact, there are companies working on that right now. That will be the moment when communications technology fulfills its ultimate potential—to connect us entirely, antiseptically and without fear of judgment or rejection, with the person we most desire.

There is only one person in the world who connects with us entirely, antiseptically, and without fear of judgment or rejection. He is at the very heart of our desire for convenience. He is at the other end of our wrist and finger. The less he needs the actual presence of other people, the more he will depend on goods and services to keep him company and populate his isolation. The more distracted and busy his isolation, the more he will measure people by their capacity to please him, or to gratify him without "getting in his face." For the only face he can bear will be his own.

ACKNOWLEDGMENTS

This book would quite simply not have been written without the moral and intellectual support of Chris Jackson. He is a brilliant, shrewd, compassionate man, a powerfully intuitive and gratifyingly unsparing editor, and a fearless advocate for (seemingly) hopeless causes. I can only thank him over time. Chris's remarkable assistant, Mya Spalter, has been of inestimable help and so has the intrepid Lucy Silag.

Cindy Spiegel and Julie Grau have created a precious pocket of oxygen in the wavering ecology of book publishing. They invited me into their atmosphere, where I breathed deeply and freely. I am grateful for the faith that these two valiant, incomparable publishers have in me.

It might seem unnatural, or perverse, or even scandalous for an author to love his agent, but I love Gloria Loomis. She protects her authors' interests as if it were a question of human rights.

A chain of events led up to and ran through the writing of this book. Along the way many people offered insights, inspiration, or encouragement that was vital: Adam Begley, Pam and Tim Brogan (and Jessica), David Bromwich, Susan Crile, John Donatich, Amanda Fortini, John and Gail Gillham (and Drake, Carson, and Victoria), Kevin Goering, Nick Goldberg, David Greenberg and Suzanne Nossel, Zoe and Steve James, Alison Karasz, Alice Quinn and Laurie Kerr, Adam and Remy Kirsch, James Lasdun, Jackson Lears, Norman Mailer, Mike Miller and Sarah Paul, Silvana Paternostro, Samantha Power, Stephanie Regis, David Rieff, Tony Scott, Rachel Shteir, Deborah Solomon and Kent Sepkowitz, Alex Star, Gitte and Theo Theodossi, Meline Toumani, Bob Weil, Marie Winn and Alan Miller. Thank you, all.

I am happy and proud to be the regular beneficiary of Janet Malcolm's integrity and wit. Edwin Frank's friendship is a constant source of fortitude and his conversation a font of rich ideas and perceptions.

To my wondrous wife, Christina Gillham, and my magical son, Julian Siegel, words cannot express what you mean to me in this life.